Commentaries On the Constitution of the United States of America

Reprefentatives and direct taxes fhall be apportioned among the feveral ftates which may be included within this union, according to their refpective numbers, which fhall be determined by adding to the whole number of free perfons, including thofe bound to fervice for a term of years, and excluding Indians not taxed, three fifths of all other perfons. The actual enumeration fhall be made within three years after the firft meeting of the congrefs of the United States, and within every fubfequent term of ten years, in fuch manner as they fhall by law direct. The number of reprefentatives fhall not exceed one for every thirty thoufand, but each ftate fhall have at leaft one reprefentative; and until fuch enumeration fhall be made, the ftate of New-Hampfhire fhall be entitled to chufe three, Maffachufetts eight, Rhode-Ifland and Providence Plantations one, Connecticut five, New-York fix, New-Jerfey four, Pennfylvania eight, Delaware one, Maryland fix, Virginia ten, North Carolina five, South-Carolina five, and Georgia three.

When vacancies happen in the reprefentation from any ftate, the executive authority thereof fhall iffue writs of election, to fill fuch vacancies.

The houfe of reprefentatives fhall choofe their fpeaker and other officers; and fhall have the fole power of impeachment.

Sect. 3. The fenate of the United States fhall be compofed of two fenators from each ftate, chofen by the legiflature thereof, for fix years; and each fenator fhall have one vote.

Immediately after they fhall be affembled in confequence of the firft election, they fhall be divided as equally as may be into three claffes. The feats of the fenators of the firft clafs fhall be vacated at the expiration of the fecond year, of the fecond clafs at the expiration of the fourth year, and of the third clafs at the expiration of the fixth year, fo that one third may be chofen every fecond year; and if vacancies happen by refignation, or otherwife, during the recefs of the legiflature of any ftate, the executive thereof may make temporary appointments until the next meeting of the legiflature, which fhall then fill fuch vacancies.

No perfon fhall be a fenator who fhall not have attained to the age of thirty years, and been nine years a citizen of the United States, and who fhall not, when elected, be an inhabitant of that ftate for which he fhall be chofen.

The Vice-President of the United States shall be President of the Senate, but shall have no vote, unless they be equally divided.

The Senate shall chuse their other officers, and also a President pro tempore, in the absence of the Vice-President, or when he shall exercise the office of President of the United States.

The senate shall have the sole power to try all impeachments. When sitting for that purpose, they shall be on oath or affirmation. When the president of the United States is tried, the chief justice shall preside: And no person shall be convicted without the concurrence of two-thirds of the members present.

Judgment in cases of impeachment shall not extend further than to removal from office, and disqualification to hold and enjoy any office of honor, trust or profit under the United States; but the party convicted shall nevertheless be liable and subject to indictment, trial, judgment and punishment, according to law.

Sect. 4. The times, places and manner of holding elections for senators and representatives, shall be prescribed in each state by the legislature thereof; but the congress may at any time by law make or alter such regulations, except as to the places for chusing senators.

The congress shall assemble at least once in every year, and such meeting shall be on the first Monday in December, unless they shall by law appoint a different day.

Sect. 5. Each house shall be the judge of elections, returns and qualifications of its own members, and a majority of each shall constitute a quorum to do business; but a smaller number may adjourn from day to day, and may be authorised to compel the attendance of absent members, in such manner, and under such penalties, as each house may provide.

Each house may determine the rules of its proceedings, punish its members for disorderly behaviour, and with the concurrence of two-thirds, expel a member.

Each house shall keep a journal of its proceedings, and from time to time publish the same, excepting such parts as may in their judgment require secrecy: and the yeas and nays of the members of either house on any question shall, at the desire of one-fifth of those present, be entered on the journal.

Neither house, during the session of congress, shall

out the consent of the other, adjourn for more than three days, nor to any other place than that in which the two houses shall be sitting.

Sect. 6. The senators and representatives shall receive a compensation for their services, to be ascertained by law, and paid out of the treasury of the United States. They shall in all cases, except treason, felony, and breach of the peace, be privileged from arrest, during the attendance at the session of their respective houses, and in going to and returning from the same; and for any speech or debate in either house, they shall not be questioned in any other place.

No senator or representative shall, during the time for which he was elected, be appointed to any civil office under the authority of the United States, which shall have been created, or the emoluments whereof shall have been encreased during such time; and no person holding any office under the United States, shall be a member of either house, during his continuance in office.

Sect. 7. All bills for raising revenue shall originate in the house of representatives; but the senate may propose or concur with amendments as on other bills.

Every bill which shall have passed the house of representatives and the senate, shall, before it become a law, be presented to the President of the United States; if he approve he shall sign it, but if not he shall return it, with his objections, to that house in which it shall have originated, who shall enter the objections at large on their journal, and proceed to reconsider it. If after such reconsideration, two-thirds of that house shall agree to pass the bill, it shall be sent, together with the objections, to the other house, by which it shall likewise be reconsidered, and if approved by two-thirds of that house, it shall become a law. But in all such cases, the votes of both houses shall be determined by yeas and nays, and the names of the persons voting for and against the bill shall be entered on the journal of each house respectively. If any bill shall not be returned by the president within ten days (Sundays excepted) after it shall have been presented to him, the same shall be a law, in like manner as if he had signed it, unless the congress, by their adjournment, prevent its return, in which case it shall not be a law.

Every order, resolution, or vote to which the concurrence of the senate and house of Representatives may be necessary (except on a question of adjournment) shall be presented to the president of the United States; and before the same shall take effect, shall be approved by him, or, being disapproved by him, shall be re-passed by two-thirds of the senate and house of representatives, according to the rules and limitations prescribed in the case of a bill.

Sect. 8. The congress shall have power

To lay and collect taxes, duties, imposts, and excises, to pay the debts, and provide for the common defence and the general welfare of the United States; but all duties, imposts and excises, shall be uniform throughout the United States;

To borrow money on the credit of the United States;

To regulate commerce with foreign nations, and among the several states, and with the Indian tribes;

To establish an uniform rule of naturalization, and uniform laws on the subject of bankruptcies throughout the United States;

To coin money, to regulate the value thereof, and of foreign coin, and fix the standard of weights and measures;

To provide for the punishment of counterfeiting the securities and current coin of the United States;

To establish post offices and post roads;

To promote the progress of science and useful arts, by securing for limited times to authors and inventors, the exclusive right to their respective writings and discoveries;

To constitute tribunals, inferior to the supreme court;

To define and punish piracies and felonies, committed on the high seas, and offences against the law of nations;

To declare war, grant letters of marque and reprisal, and make rules concerning captures on land and water;

To raise and support armies, but no appropriation of money to that use, shall be for a longer term than two years;

To provide and maintain a navy;

To make rules for the government and regulation of the land and naval forces;

To provide for calling forth the militia, to execute the laws of the union, suppress insurrections, and repel invasions;

To provide for organizing, arming, and disciplining the militia, and for governing such part of them as may be employed in the service of the United States, reserving to the states respectively, the appointment of the officers, and the authority of training the militia, according to the discipline prescribed by congress;

To exercise exclusive legislation in all cases whatsoever, over such district (not exceeding ten miles square) as may, by cession of particular states, and the acceptance of congress, become the seat of government of the United States; and to exercise like authority over all places purchased by the consent of the legislature of the state in which the same shall be, for the erection of forts, magazines, arsenals, dock-yards, and other needful buildings; and

To make all laws which shall be necessary and proper for carrying into execution the foregoing powers, and all other powers vested by this constitution in the government of the United States, or in any department or officer thereof.

Sect. 9. The migration or importation of such persons as any of the states now existing shall think proper to admit, shall not be prohibited by congress prior to the year one thousand eight hundred and eight; but a tax or duty may be imposed on such importation, not exceeding ten dollars for each person.

The privilege of the writ of habeas corpus shall not be suspended, unless when in cases of rebellion, or invasion, the public safety may require it.

No bill of attainder, or ex post facto law shall be passed.

No capitation, or other direct tax shall be laid, unless in proportion to the census or enumeration herein before directed to be taken.

No tax or duty shall be laid on articles exported from any state. No preference shall be given by any regulation of commerce or revenue to the ports of one state over those of another: nor shall vessels bound to, or from, one state, be obliged to enter, clear, or pay duties in another.

No money shall be drawn from the treasury, but in consequence of appropriations made by law; and a regular statement and account of the receipts and expenditures of all public money shall be published from time to time.

No title of nobility shall be granted by the United States: And no person holding any office of profit or trust under them, shall, without the consent of congress, accept of any present, emolument, office, or title, of any kind whatever, from any king, prince, or foreign state.

Sect. 10. No state shall enter into any treaty, alliance, or confederation; grant letters of marque and reprisal; coin money; emit bills of credit; make any thing but gold and silver coin a tender in payment of debts; pass any bill of

attainder, ex post facto law, or law impairing the obligation of contracts, or grant any title of nobility.

No state shall, without the consent of congress, lay any impost or duties on imports or exports, except what may be absolutely necessary for executing its inspection laws; and the net produce of all duties and imposts, laid by any state on imports or exports, shall be for the use of the treasury of the United States; and all such laws shall be subject to the revision and controul of the congress. No state shall, without the consent of congress, lay any duty of tonnage, keep troops, or ships of war in time of peace, enter into any agreement or compact with another state, or with a foreign power, or engage in war, unless actually invaded, or in such imminent danger as will not admit of delay.

ARTICLE II.

Sect. 1. The executive power shall be vested in a president of the United States of America. He shall hold his office during the term of four years, and, together with the vice-president, chosen for the same term, be elected as follows:

Each state shall appoint, in such manner as the legislature thereof may direct, a number of electors, equal to the whole number of senators and representatives to which the state may be entitled in the congress: but no senator or representative, or person holding any office of trust or profit under the United States, shall be appointed an elector.

The electors shall meet in their respective states, and vote by ballot for two persons, of whom one at least shall not be an inhabitant of the same state with themselves. And they shall make a list of all the persons voted for, and of the number of votes for each; which list they shall sign and certify, and transmit sealed to the seat of government of the United States, directed to the president of the senate. The president of the senate shall, in the presence of the senate and house of representatives, open all the certificates, and the votes shall then be counted. The person having the greatest number of votes shall be the president, if such number be a majority of the whole number of electors ap pointed; and if there be more than one who have such jority, and have an equal number of votes, then the of repres hall immediately chuse by ballot them for prefident; and if no perfon have a majority, then from the five higheft on the lift the faid houfe fhall in like manner chufe the prefident. But in chufing the prefident, the votes fhall be taken by ftates, the reprefentation from each ftate having one vote; a quorum for this purpofe fhall confift of a member or members from two thirds of the ftates, and a majority of the ftates fhall be neceffary to a choice. In every cafe, after the choice of the prefident, the perfon having the greateft number of votes of the electors fhall be the vice-prefident. But if there fhould remain two or more who have equal votes, the fenate fhall chufe from them, by ballot, the vice-prefident.

The congrefs may determine the time of chufing the electors, and the day on which they fhall give their votes; which day fhall be the fame throughout the United States.

No perfon except a natural born citizen, or a citizen of the United States, at the time of the adoption of this conftitution, fhall be eligible to the office of prefident; neither fhall any perfon be eligible to that office who fhall not have attained to the age of thirty-five years, and been fourteen years a refident within the United States.

In cafe of the removal of the prefident from office, or of his death, refignation, or inability to difcharge the powers and duties of the faid office, the fame fhall devolve on the vice-prefident, and the congrefs may by law provide for the cafe of removal, death, refignation or inability, both of the prefident, and vice-prefident, declaring what officer fhall then act as prefident, and fuch officer fhall act accordingly, until the difability be removed, or a prefident fhall be elected.

The prefident fhall, at ftated times, receive for his fervices, a compenfation, which fhall neither be encreafed nor diminifhed during the period for which he fhall have been elected, and he fhall not receive, within that period, any other emolument from the United States, or any of them.

Before he enter on the execution of his office, he fhall take the following oath or affirmation :

" I do folemnly fwear (or affirm) that I will faithfully execute the office of prefident of the United States, and will, beft of my ability, preferve, protect and defend the tion of the United States."

2. The prefident fhall be commander in chief of my and navy of the United States, and of the militia ſe feveral ftates, when called into the actual fervice

of the United States; he may require the opinion, in writing, of the principal officer in each of the executive departments, upon any subject relating to the duties of their respective offices, and he shall have power to grant reprieves and pardons for offences against the United States, except in cases of impeachment.

He shall have power, by and with the advice and consent of the senate, to make treaties, provided two-thirds of the senators present concur; and he shall nominate, and by and with the advice and consent of the senate, shall appoint ambassadors, other public ministers and consuls, judges of the supreme court, and all other officers of the United States, whose appointments are not herein otherwise provided for, and which shall be established by law. But the congress may by law vest the appointment of such inferior officers, as they think proper, in the president alone, in the courts of law, or in the heads of departments.

The president shall have power to fill up all vacancies that may happen during the recess of the senate, by granting commissions which shall expire at the end of their next session.

Sect. 3. He shall from time to time give to the congress information of the state of the union, and recommend to their consideration such measures as he shall judge necessary and expedient; he may, on extraordinary occasions, convene both houses, or either of them, and in case of disagreement between them, with respect to the time of adjournment, he may adjourn them to such time as he shall think proper; he shall receive ambassadors and other public ministers; he shall take care that the laws be faithfully executed; and shall commission all the officers of the United States.

Sect. 4. The president, vice-president and all civil officers of the United States, shall be removed from office on impeachment for, and conviction of, treason, bribery, or other high crimes and misdemeanors.

ARTICLE III.

Sect. 1. The judicial power of the United States, shall be vested in one supreme court, and in such inferior courts as the congress may from time to time ordain and establish. The judges, both of the supreme and inferior courts, shall hold their offices during good behaviour, and shall, at stated times, receive for their services; a compensation, which shall not be diminished during their continuance in office.

Sect. 2. The judicial power shall extend to all cases, in law and equity, arising under this constitution, the laws of the United States, and treaties made, or which shall be made, under their authority; to all cases affecting ambassadors, other public ministers and consuls; in all cases of admiralty and maritime jurisdiction; to controversies to which the United States shall be a party; to controversies between two or more states, between a state and citizens of another state, between citizens of different states, between citizens of the same state claiming lands under grants of different states, and between a state, or the citizens thereof, and foreign states, citizens or subjects.

In all cases affecting ambassadors, other public ministers and consuls, and those in which a state shall be party, the supreme court shall have original jurisdiction. In all the other cases before mentioned the supreme court shall have appellate jurisdiction, both as to law and fact, with such exceptions, and under such regulations, as the congress shall make.

The trial of all crimes, except in case of impeachment, shall be by jury; and such trial shall be held in the state where the said crimes shall have been committed; but when not committed within any state, the trial shall be at such place or places as the congress may, by law have directed.

Sect. 3. Treason against the United States shall consist only in levying war against them, or in adhering to their enemies, giving them aid and comfort. No person shall be convicted of treason, unless on the testimony of two witnesses to the same overt act, or on confession in open court.

The congress shall have power to declare the punishment of treason, but no attainder of treason shall work corruption of blood, or forfeiture, except during the life of the person attainted.

ARTICLE IV.

Sect. 1. Full faith and credit shall be given in each state to the public acts, records, and judicial proceedings of every other state. And the congress may by general laws prescribe the manner in which such acts, records, and proceedings shall be proved, and the effect thereof.

Sect. 2. The citizens of each state shall be entitled to all privileges and immunities of citizens in the several states.

A person charged in any state with treason, felony, or other crime, who shall flee from justice, and be found in another state, shall, on demand of the executive authority of the state from which he fled be delivered up, to be removed to the state having jurisdiction of the crime.

No person held to service or labour in one state, under the laws thereof, escaping into another, shall, in consequence of any law or regulation therein, be discharged from such service or labour, but shall be delivered up on claim of the party to whom such service or labour may be due.

Sect. 3. New states may be admitted by the congress into this union; but no new state shall be formed or erected within the jurisdiction of any other state; nor any state be formed by the junction of two or more states, or parts of states, without the consent of the legislatures of the states concerned, as well as of the congress.

The congress shall have power to dispose of and make all needful rules and regulations respecting the territory or other property belonging to the United States; and nothing in this constitution shall be so construed as to prejudice any claims of the United States, or of any particular state.

Sect. 4. The United States shall guarantee to every state in this union, a republican form of government, and shall protect each of them against invasion; and on application of the legislature, or of the executive (when the legislature cannot be convened) against domestic violence.

ARTICLE V.

The Congress, whenever two-thirds of both houses shall deem it necessary, shall propose amendments to this Constitution, or, on the application of the legislature of two-thirds of the several states, shall call a convention for proposing amendments, which, in either case, shall be valid to all intents and purposes, as part of this constitution, when ratified by the legislatures of three-fourths of the several states, or by conventions in three-fourths thereof, as the one or the other mode of ratification may be proposed by the Congress; Provided, that no amendment which may be made prior to the year one thousand eight hundred and eight shall in any manner affect the first and fourth clauses in the ninth section of the first article; and that no state, without its consent, shall be deprived of its equal suffrage in the senate.

ARTICLE VI.

All debts contracted, and engagements entered into, before the adoption of this constitution, shall be as valid against the United States, under this constitution, as under the confederation.

This constitution, and the laws of the United States which shall be made in pursuance thereof, and all treaties made, or which shall be made, under the authority of the United States, shall be the supreme law of the land; and the judges in every state shall be bound thereby; any thing in the constitution or laws of any state to the contrary notwithstanding.

The senators and representatives before-mentioned, and the members of the several state legislatures, and all executive and judicial officers, both of the United States and of the several states, shall be bound by oath or affirmation, to support this constitution: but no religious test shall ever be required as a qualification to any office or public trust under the United States.

ARTICLE VII.

The ratification of the conventions of nine states, shall be sufficient for the establishment of this constitution between the states so ratifying the same.

DONE in CONVENTION, by the unanimous consent of the states present, the seventeenth day of September, in the year of our Lord one thousand seven hundred and eighty seven, and of the Independence of the United States of America the twelfth. In witness whereof we have hereunto subscribed our names.

GEORGE WASHINGTON, President,
and Deputy from Virginia.

NEW-HAMPSHIRE.
John Langdon,
Nicholas Gilman.

MASSACHUSETTS.
Nathaniel Gorham,
Rufus King.

CONNECTICUT.
William Samuel Johnson,
Roger Sherman.

NEW-YORK.
ilton.
ey.
ton,

PENNSYLVANIA.
Benjamin Franklin,
Thomas Mifflin,
Robert Morris,
George Clymer,
Thomas Fitzsimons,
Jared Ingersoll,
James Wilson,
Gouverneur Morris.

DELAWARE.
George Read,
Gunning Bedford, jun.
John Dickinson,
Richard Bassett,
Jacob Broom.

MARYLAND.
James McHenry,
Daniel of St. Thomas Jenifer,
Daniel Carrol.
VIRGINIA.
John Blair,
James Madison, jun.
NORTH-CAROLINA.
William Blount,
Richard Dobbs Spaight,

Hugh Williamson.
SOUTH-CAROLINA.
John Rutledge,
Charles Cotesworth Pinckney,
Charles Pinckney,
Pierce Butler.
GEORGIA.
William Few,
Abraham Baldwin.

ATTEST. WILLIAM JACKSON, *Secretary.*

In CONVENTION, Monday, September 17th, 1787.

RESOLVED,

THAT the preceding constitution be laid before the United States in congress assembled, and that it is the opinion of this convention, that it should afterwards be submitted to a convention of delegates, chosen in each state by the people thereof, under the recommendation of its legislature, for their assent and ratification; and that each convention assenting to, and ratifying the same, should give notice thereof to the United States in congress assembled.

RESOLVED, That it is the opinion of this convention, that as soon as the conventions of nine states shall have ratified this constitution, the United States in congress assembled should fix a day on which electors should be appointed by the states which shall have ratified the same, and a day on which the electors should assemble to vote for the president, and the time and place for commencing proceedings under this constitution. That after such publication the electors should be appointed, and the senators and representatives elected: That the electors should meet on the day fixed for the election of the president, and should transmit their votes certified, signed, sealed and directed, as the constitution requires, to the secretary of the United States in congress assembled; that the senators and representatives should convene at the time and place assigned; that the senators should appoint a president of the senate, for the sole purpose of receiving, opening and counting the votes for president; and, that after he should be chosen, the congrefs, together with the prefident, fhould, without delay, proceed to execute this conftitution.

By the unanimous order of the Convention,

GEORGE WASHINGTON, *Prefident.*
William Jackfon, Secretary.

In CONVENTION, September 17th, 1787.

SIR,

WE have now the honor to fubmit to the confideration of the United States in congrefs affembled, the conftitution which has appeared to us the moft advifeable.

The friends of our country have long feen and defired, that the power of making war, peace and treaties, that of levying money and regulating commerce, and the correfpondent, executive, and judicial authorities, fhould be fully and effectually vefted in the general government of the union; but the impropriety of delegating fuch extenfive truft to one body of men is evident---Hence refults the neceffity of a different organization.

It is obvioufly impracticable in the fœderal government of thefe ftates, to fecure all rights of independent fovereignty to each, and yet provide for the intereft and fafety of all--- Individuals entering into fociety, muft give up a fhare of liberty to preferve the reft. The magnitude of the facrifice muft depend as well on fituation and circumftance, as on the object to be obtained. It is at all times difficult to draw with precifion the line between thofe rights which muft be furrendered, and thofe which may be referved; and on the prefent occafion this difficulty was encreafed by a difference among the feveral ftates as to their fituation, extent, habits, and particular interefts.

In all our deliberations on this fubject, we kept fteadily in our view, that which appears to us the greateft intereft of every true American, the confolidation of our union, in which is involved our profperity, felicity, fafety, perhaps our national exiftence. This important confideration, ferioufly and deeply impreffed on our minds, led each ftate in the convention to be lefs rigid on points of inferior magnitude, than might have been otherwife expected; and thus the conftitution, which we now prefent, is the refult of a fpirit of amity, and of that mutual deference and conceffion which the peculiarity of our political situation rendered indispensible.

That it will meet the full and entire approbation of every state is not perhaps to be expected; but each will doubtless consider, that had her interests been alone consulted, the consequences might have been particularly disagreeable or injurious to others; that it is liable to as few exceptions as could reasonably have been expected, we hope and believe; that it may promote the lasting welfare of that country so dear to us all, and secure her freedom and happiness, is our most ardent wish.----With great respect, we have the honor to be, sir, your excellency's most obedient and humble servants.

GEORGE WASHINGTON, *President*.

By the unanimous order of the Convention.

His Excellency the President of Congress.

COMMENTARIES

ON THE

CONSTITUTION

OF THE

UNITED STATES OF AMERICA.

THE Convention of the People of the State of Pennsylvania being duly organized on the 21ſt of November, 1787, proceeded to the conſideration of the New Conſtitution propoſed by the General Convention of Delegates from twelve of the thirteen United States—for the acceptance of the people of the individual States; and on the 26th, having read that inſtrument twice over, a debate commenced, from which are extracted the following ſpeeches, forming, as it were, a complete comment and diſſertation upon the ſubject of a Republican Government.

It may, however, not be amiſs in us to remark, previous to entering on our extracts, that the opponents to the new ſyſtem of government * were urgent in ſtating immediately their objections, which were reducible to the following points:

* Mr. Findley, Mr. Smilie, and Mr. Whitehill.

(21)

There is no declaration of rights in this Conſtitution, and the laws of the general government being paramount to the laws and conſtitutions of the ſeveral States, the declarations of rights in the ſeveral ſtate conſtitutions are no ſecurity—nor are the people ſecured even in the enjoyment of the benefits of the common law.

Owing to the ſmall number of Members in the Houſe of Repreſentatives, there is not the ſubſtance, but the ſhadow only of repreſentation, which can never produce proper information in the Legiſlature, or inſpire confidence in the people—the laws will therefore be generally made by men little concerned in, and unacquainted with, their effects and conſequences.

The Senate have the power of altering all money bills, and of originating appropriations of money, although they are not the immediate repreſentatives of the people, or amenable to them, theſe and their other great powers, viz. their power in the appointment of Ambaſſadors, and all public officers, in making treaties, and trying all impeachments; their influence upon, and connection with, the ſupreme executive. From theſe circumſtances, their duration of office, and their being a conſtant exiſting body, almoſt continually ſitting, joined with their being one complete branch of the Legiſlature, will deſtroy any and every balance in the government, and enable them to accompliſh what uſurpation they pleaſe upon the rights and liberties of the people.

The Judiciary of the United States is ſo conſtructed and extended as to abſorb and deſtroy the Judiciaries of the ſeveral States, thereby rendering law as *tedious, intricate, and expenſive,* and juſtice as *unattainable,* by a great part of the community, as ', and enabling the rich to oppreſs and ruin the

The

The President of the United States has no conftitutional Council—a thing unknown in any fafe and regular Government—he will therefore be unfupported by proper information and advice, and will generally be directed by minions and favourites, or he will become a tool to the Senate, or a Council of State will grow out of the principal officers of the great departments, the worft and moft dangerous of all ingredients for fuch a Council in a free country ; for they may be induced to join in any dangerous or oppreffive meafures to fhelter themfelves, and prevent an inquiry into their own mifconduct in office: whereas, had a conftitutional Council been formed, as was faid to have been propofed, of fix Members, viz. two from the Eaftern, two from the Middle, and two from the Southern States, to be appointed by vote of the States in the Houfe of Reprefentatives, with the fame duration and rotation of office as the Senate, the executive would always have had fafe and proper information and advice ; the Prefident of fuch a Council might have acted as Vice Prefident of the United States, *pro tempore*, upon any vacancy or difability of the Chief Magiftrate, and the long-continued feffions of the Senate would, in a great meafure, have been prevented. From this fatal defect of a conftitutional Council has arifen the improper power of the Senate in the appointment of public officers, and the alarming dependence and connection between that branch of the legiflature and the executive. Hence alfo fprung that unneceffary and dangerous office of the Vice Prefident, who, for want of other employment, is made Prefident of the Senate, thereby dangeroufly blending the legiflative and executive powers ; befides always giving to fome one of the States an unneceffary and unjuft pre-eminence over the others.

The Prefident of the United States has the unreftrained power of granting pardon for treafons, which may be fometimes exercifed to fcreen from punifhment thofe whom he had

fecretly

secretly instigated to commit the crime, and thereby prevent the discovery of his own guilt.

By declaring all treaties supreme laws of the land, the executive and senate have, in many cases, an exclusive power of legislation, which might have been avoided by proper distinctions with respect to treaties, and requiring the assent of the House of Representatives, were it could be done with safety.

Under their own construction of the general clause at the end of the enumerated powers, the Congress may grant monopolies in trade and commerce—constitute new crimes—inflict unusual and severe punishments, and extend their power as far as they shall think proper—so that the State Legislatures have no security for the powers now presumed to remain to them, or the people for their rights.

There is no declaration for preserving the liberty of the press, the trial by jury in civil causes, nor against the danger of standing armies in time of peace.

Mr. M'KEAN said, there was an indiscreet haste in running so immediately into the particular examination of the several parts of the system; although he admitted that the subject generally was fully and fairly before them. Our first object, Mr. President, (said he) must be to ascertain the proper mode of proceeding to obtain a final decision. We are without precedent to guide us; yet those forms, observed by other public bodies, so far as they are eligible, may generally be proper for us to adhere to. So far, therefore, as the rules of the Legislature of Pennsylvania apply with convenience to our circumstance, I acquiesce in their adoption.

I now think it necessary, Sir, to make you a motion, not that I apprehend it can be determined until a full investigation of the subject before us has taken place. This motion will be, Sir, That this convention do *assent to* and *ratify* the constitution agreed to on the 17th of September last, by the convention of the United States of America, held at Philadelphia.

Upon this motion being seconded, sir, the consideration of the constitution will be necessarily drawn on. Every objection that can be suggested against the work, will be listened to with attention, answered, and perhaps obviated. And finally, after a full discussion, the ground will be ascertained, on which we are to receive or reject the system now before you. I do not wish this question to be decided to day; tho' perhaps it may be determined this day week. I offer you this for the sake of form, and shall hereafter trouble you with another motion, that may bring the particular parts of this constitution before you, for a regular and satisfactory investigation.

In this motion, Mr. M'Kean was seconded by Mr. Allison.

MR. WILSON.

The system proposed, by the late convention, for the government of the United States, is now before you. Of that convention I had the honor to be a member. As I am the only member of that body, who have the honor to be also a member of this, it may be expected that I should prepare the way for the deliberations of this assembly, by unfolding the difficulties, which the late convention were obliged to encounter; by pointing out the end, which they proposed to accomplish, and by tracing the general principles, which they have adopted for the accomplishment of that end.

To form a good system of government for a single city or state, however limited as to territory, or inconsiderable as to numbers, has been thought to require the strongest efforts of human genius. With what conscious diffidence, then, must the members of the convention have revolved in their minds the immense undertaking, which was before them. Their views could not be confined to a small or a single community, but were expanded to a great number of states; several of which contain an extent of territory, and resources of population, equal to those of some of the most respectable kingdoms on the other side of the Atlantic. Nor were even these the only objects to be comprehended within their deliberations. Numerous states yet unformed: Myriads of the human race, who will inhabit regions hitherto uncultivated, were to be affected by the result of their proceedings. It was necessary, therefore, to form their calculations on a scale commensurate to a large portion of the globe.

D

For my own part, I have been often loft in aftonifhment at the vaftnefs of the profpect before us. To open the navigation of a fingle river was lately thought in Europe, an enterprize adequate to imperial glory. But could the commercial fcenes of the Scheldt be compared with thofe, that, under a good government, will be exhibited on the Hudfon, the Delaware, the Potowmac, and the numerous other rivers, that water and are intended to enrich the dominions of the United States?

The difficulty of the bufinefs was equal to its magnitude. No fmall fhare of wifdom and addrefs is requifite to combine and reconcile the jarring interefts, that prevail, or feem to prevail, in a fingle community. The United States contain already thirteen governments mutually independent. Thofe governments prefent to the Atlantic a front of fifteen hundred miles in extent. Their foil, their climates, their productions, their dimenfions, their numbers are different.—In many inftances a difference and even an oppofition fubfifts among their interefts: And a difference and even an oppofition is imagined to fubfift in many more. An apparent intereft produces the fame attachment as a real one; and is often purfued with no lefs perfeverance and vigour. When all thefe circumftances are feen and attentively confidered, will any member of this honorable body be furprized, that fuch a diverfity of things produced a proportioned diverfity of fentiment? Will he be furprized that fuch a diverfity of fentiment rendered a fpirit of mutual forbearance and conciliation indifpenfably neceffary to the fuccefs of the great work? and will he be furprized that mutual conceffions and facrifices were the confequences of mutual forbearance and conciliation? When the fprings of oppofition were fo numerous and ftrong, and poured forth their waters in courfes fo varying, need we be furprized that the ftream formed by their conjunction, was impelled in a direction fomewhat different from that, which each of them would have taken feparately?

I have reafon to think that a difficulty arofe in the minds of fome members of convention from another confideration—their ideas of the temper and difpofition of the people, for whom the conftitution is propofed. The citizens of the United States, however different in fome other refpects, are well known to agree in one ftrongly marked feature of their character—a warm and keen fenfe of freedom and independence. This fenfe has been heightened by the glorious refult of their late ſtruggle againſt all the efforts of one of the moſt powerful nations of Europe. It was apprehended, I believe, by ſome, that a people ſo highly ſpirited, would ill brook the reſtraints of an efficient government. I confeſs that this conſideration did not influence my conduct. I knew my conſtituents to be high-ſpirited, but I knew them alſo to poſſeſs ſound ſenſe. I knew that, in the event, they would be beſt pleaſed with that ſyſtem of government, which would be beſt promote their freedom and happineſs. I have often revolved this ſubject in my mind. I have ſuppoſed one of my conſtituents to aſk me, why I gave ſuch a vote on a particular queſtion? I have always thought it would be a ſatisfactory anſwer to ſay, becauſe I judged, upon the beſt conſideration I could give, that ſuch a vote was right. I have thought that it would be but a very poor compliment to my conſtituents to ſay—that, in my opinion, ſuch a vote would have been proper, but that I ſuppoſed a contrary one would be more agreeable to thoſe who ſent me to the convention. I could not, even in idea, expoſe myſelf to ſuch a retort, as, upon the laſt anſwer, might have been juſtly made to me. Pray, ſir, what reaſons have you for ſuppoſing that a right vote would diſpleaſe your conſtituents? is this the proper return for the high confidence they have placed in you? If they have given cauſe for ſuch a ſurmiſe, it was by chooſing a repreſentative, who could entertain ſuch an opinion of them. I was under no apprehenſion that the good people of this ſtate would behold, with diſpleaſure, the brightneſs of the rays of delegated power, when it only proved the ſuperior ſplendor of the luminary, of which thoſe rays were only the reflexion.

A very important difficulty aroſe from comparing the extent of the country to be governed, with the kind of government which it would be proper to eſtabliſh in it. It has been an opinion, countenanced by high authority, "that "the natural property of ſmall ſtates is to be governed as a "republic; of middling ones, to be ſubject to a monarch; "and of large empires, to be ſwayed by a deſpotic prince; "and that the conſequence is, that, in order to preſerve the "principles of the eſtabliſhed government, the ſtate muſt be "ſupported in the extent it has acquired; and that the ſpi- "rit of the ſtate will alter in proportion as it extends or con- "tracts its limits." (Monteſquieu, b. 8. c. 20.) This opinion ſeems to be ſupported, rather than contradicted, by the hiſto-

ry of the governments in the old world. Here then the difficulty appeared in full view. On one hand, the United States contain an immense extent of territory, and, according to the foregoing opinion, a despotic government is best adapted to that extent. On the other hand, it was well known, that, however the citizens of the United States might, with pleasure, submit to the legitimate restraints of a republican constitution, they would reject, with indignation, the fetters of despotism. What then was to be done? The idea of a confederate republic presented itself. This kind of constitution has been thought to have "all the internal advanta-
"ges of a republican, together with the external force of a
"monarchical government." Mont. b. 9. c. 1. 2. Paley 199. 202.

Its description is, "a convention, by which several states
"agree to become members of a larger one, which they
"intend to establish. It is a kind of assemblage of societies,
"that constitute a *new one*, capable of encreasing by means of
"farther association." Montesquieu, b. 9. c. 1. The *expanding* quality of such a government is peculiarly fitted for the United States, the greatest part of whose territory is yet uncultivated.

But while this form of government enabled us to surmount the difficulty last mentioned, it conducted us to another, of which I am now to take notice. It left us almost without precedent or guide; and consequently, without the benefit of that instruction, which, in many cases, may be derived from the constitution, and history and experience of other nations. Several associations have frequently been called by the name of confederate states, which have not, in propriety of language, deserved it. The Swiss Cantons are connected only by alliances. The United Netherlands are indeed an assemblage of societies; but this assemblage constitutes *no new one*; and, therefore, it does not correspond with the full definition of a confederate republic. The Germanic body is composed of such disproportioned and discordant materials, and its structure is so intricate and complex, that little useful knowledge can be drawn from it. Ancient history discloses, and barely discloses to our view, some confederate republics—the Achaean league—the Lycian confederacy, and the Amphyctyonic council. But the facts recorded concerning their constitutions are so few and general, and their histories are so unmarked and defective, that no satisfactory information can be collected from them concerning many particular circumstances, from an accurate discernment and comparison, of which alone legitimate and practical inferences can be made from one constitution to another. Besides, the situation and dimensions of those confederacies, and the state of society, manners and habits in them, were so different from those of the United States, that the most correct descriptions could have supplied but a very small fund of applicable remark. Thus, in forming this system, we were deprived of many advantages, which the history and experience of other ages and other countries would, in other cases, have afforded us.

Permit me to add, in this place, that the science even of government itself, seems yet to be almost in its state of infancy. Governments, in general, have been the result of force, of fraud, and of accident. After a period of six thousand years has elapsed since the creation, the United States exhibit to the world, the first instance, as far as we can learn, of a nation, unattacked by external force, unconvulsed by domestic insurrections, assembling voluntarily, deliberating fully, and deciding calmly, concerning that system of government, under which they would wish that they and their posterity should live. The ancients, so enlightened on other subjects, were very uninformed with regard to this. They seem scarcely to have had any idea of any other kinds of governments, than the three simple forms, designed by the epithets, monarchical, aristocratical and democratical. I know that much and pleasing ingenuity has been exerted, in modern times, in drawing entertaining parallels between some of the ancient constitutions and some of the mixed governments that have since existed in Europe. But I much suspect that, on strict examination, the instances of resemblance will be found to be few and weak; to be suggested by the improvements, which, in subsequent ages, have been made in government, and not to be drawn immediately from the ancient constitutions themselves, as they were intended and understood by those who framed them. To illustrate this, a similar observation may be made on another subject. Admiring critics have fancied that they have discovered in their favourite *Homer* the seeds of all the improvements in philosophy and in the sciences, made since his time. What induces me to be of this opinion is, that *Tacitus*—the profound politician Tacitus—who lived towards the latter end of those ages, which are now denominated ancient, who undoubtedly had studied the constitutions of all the states and kingdoms known before and in his time; and who certainly was qualified in an uncommon degree, for understanding the full force and operation of each of them, confiders, after all he had known and read, a mixed government, composed of the three simple forms, as a thing rather to be wished than expected: And he thinks, that if such a government could even be instituted, its duration could not be long. One thing is very certain, that the doctrine of representation in government was altogether unknown to the ancients. Now the knowledge and practice of this doctrine is, in my opinion, essential to every system, that can possess the qualities of freedom, wisdom and energy.

It is worthy of remark, and the remark may, perhaps, excite some surprise, that representation of the people is not, even at this day, the sole principle of any government in Europe. Great-Britain boasts, and she may well boast, of the improvement she has made in politics, by the admission of representation: For the improvement is important as far as it goes: but it by no means goes far enough. Is the executive power of Great-Britain founded on representation? This is not pretended. Before the revolution many of the kings claimed to reign by divine right, and others by hereditary right; and even at the revolution, nothing farther was affected or attempted, than the recognition of certain parts of an original contract*, supposed, at some former remote period, to have been made between the king and the people. A contract seems to exclude, rather than to imply, delegated power. The judges of Great-Britain are appointed by the crown. The judicial authority, therefore, does not depend upon representation, even in its most remote degree. Does representation prevail in the legislative department of the British government? even here it does not predominate; though it may serve as a check. The legislature consists of three branches, the king, the lords, and the commons. Of these only the latter are supported by the constitution to represent the authority of the people. This short analysis clearly shews to what a narrow corner of the British constitution the principle of representation is confined. I believe it does not extend farther, if so far in any other government in Europe. For the American states, were reserved the glory and the happiness of diffusing this vital principle throughout the constituent parts of government. Representation is the chain of communication between the people, and those, to whom they

* Blackstone, 233.

have committed the exercise of the powers of government. This chain may consist of one or more links; but in all cases it should be sufficiently strong and discernable.

To be left without guide or precedent was not the only difficulty, in which the convention were involved, by proposing to their constituents a plan of a confederate republic. They found themselves embarrassed with another of peculiar delicacy and importance; I mean that of drawing a proper line between the national government, and the government of the several states. It was easy to discover a proper and satisfactory principle on the subject. Whatever object of government is confined in its operation and effects within the bounds of a particular state, should be considered as belonging to the government of that state; whatever object of government extends in its operation or effects beyond the bounds of a particular state, should be considered as belonging to the government of the United States; but though this principle be found and satisfactory, its application to particular cases would be accompanied with much difficulty; because in its application, room must be allowed for great discretionary latitude of construction of the principle. In order to lessen, or remove the difficulty, arising from discretionary construction on this subject, an enumeration of particular instances, in which the application of the principle ought to take place, has been attempted with much industry and care. It is only in mathematical science that a line can be described with mathematical precision. But I flatter myself that upon the strictest investigation, the enumeration will be found to be safe and unexceptionable; and accurate too in as great a degree as accuracy can be expected in a subject of this nature. Particulars under this head will be more properly explained, when we descend to the minute view of the enumeration, which is made in the proposed constitution.

After all, it will be necessary, that, on a subject so peculiarly delicate as this, much prudence, much candour, much moderation and much liberality, should be exercised and displayed both by the fœderal government and by the governments of the several states. It is to be hoped, that those virtues in government will be exercised and displayed, when we consider, that the powers of the fœderal government and those of the state governments are drawn from sources equally pure. If a difference can be discovered between them, it is in favor of the fœderal government, because that government is founded on a reprefentation of the *whole* union; whereas the government of any particular ftate is founded only on the reprefentation of a part, inconfiderable when compared with the whole. Is it not more reafonable to fuppofe, that the counfels of the whole will embrace the intereft of every part, than that the counfels of any part will embrace the interefts of the whole?

I intend not, fir, by this defcription of the difficulties with which the convention were furrounded, to magnify their fkill or their merit in furmounting them, or to infinuate that any predicament in which the convention ftood, fhould prevent the clofeft and moft cautious fcrutiny into the performance, which they have exhibited to their conftituents and to the world. My intention is of far other and higher aim—to evince by the conflicts and difficulties which muft arife from the many and powerful caufes which I have enumerated, that it is hopelefs and impracticable to form a conftitution, which, in every part, will be acceptable to every citizen, or even to every government in the United States; and that all which can be expected is, to form fuch a conftitution, as upon the whole, is the beft that can poffibly be obtained. Man and perfection!—a ftate and perfection!—an affemblage of ftates and perfection!—can we reafonably expect, however ardently we may wifh to behold the glorious union?

I can well recollect, though I believe I cannot convey to others the impreffion, which, on many occafions, was made by the difficulties which furrounded and preffed the convention. The great undertaking, at fome times, feemed to be at a ftand, at other times, its motion feemed to be retrograde. At the conclufion, however, of our work, many of the members expreffed their aftonifhment at the fuccefs with which it terminated.

Having enumerated fome of the difficulties, which the convention were obliged to encounter in the courfe of their proceedings, I fhall next point out the end, which they propofed to accomplifh. Our wants, our talents, our affections, our paffions, all tell us that we were made for a ftate of fociety. But a ftate of fociety could not be fupported long or happily without fome civil reftraint. It is true, that, in a ftate of nature, any one individual may act uncontrolled by others; but it is equally true, that in fuch a ftate, every other individual may act uncontrolled by him. Amidft this universal independence, the dissentions and animosities between interfering members of the society, would be numerous and ungovernable. The consequence would be, that each member, in such a natural state, would enjoy less liberty, and suffer more interruption, than he would in a regulated society. Hence the universal introduction of governments of some kind or other into the social state. The liberty of every member is encreased by this introduction; for each gains more by the limitation of the freedom of every other member, than he loses by the limitation of his own. The result is, that civil government is necessary to the perfection and happiness of man. In forming this government, and carrying it into execution, it is *essential* that the *interest* and *authority* of the whole community should be binding in every part of it.

The foregoing principles and conclusions are generally admitted to be just and sound with regard to the nature and formation of single governments, and the duty of submission to them. In some cases they will apply, with much propriety and force, to states already formed. The advantages and necessity of civil government among individuals in society, are not greater or stronger than, in some situations and circumstances, are the advantages and necessity of a fœderal government among states. A natural and a very important question now presents itself---is such the situation---are such the circumstances of the United States? A proper answer to this question will unfold some very interesting truths.

The United States may adopt any one of four different systems. They may become consolidated into one government, in which the separate existence of the states shall be entirely absorbed. They may reject any plan of union or association, and act as separate and unconnected states. They may form two or more confederacies. They may unite in one fœderal republic. Which of these systems ought to have been formed by the convention? To support, with vigour, a single government over the whole extent of the United States, would demand a system of the most unqualified and the most unremitted despotism.—Such a number of separate states, contiguous in situation, unconnected and disunited in government, would be, at one time, the prey of foreign force, foreign influence, and foreign intrigue; at another, the victim of mutual rage, rancour and revenge

E

Neither of these systems found advocates in the late convention: I presume they will not find advocates in this. Would it be proper to divide the United States into two or more confederacies? It will not be unadviseable to take a more minute survey of this subject. Some aspects, under which it may be viewed, are far from being, at first sight, uninviting. Two or more confederacies would be each more compact and more manageable than a single one extending over the same territory. By dividing the United States into two or more confederacies, the great collision of interests, apparently or really different and contrary, in the *whole extent* of their dominion, would be broken, and, in a great measure, disappear in the several parts. But these disadvantages, which are discovered from certain points of view, are greatly overbalanced by inconveniences that will appear on a more accurate examination. Animosities, and, perhaps wars, would arise from assigning the extent, the limits, and the rights of the different confederacies. The expences of governing would be multiplied by the number of foederal governments. The danger resulting from foreign influence and mutual dissentions, would not, perhaps, be less great and alarming in the instance of different confederacies, than in the instance of different though more numerous unassociated states. These observations, and many others that might be made on the subject, will be sufficient to evince, that a division of the United States into a number of separate confederacies, would probably be an unsatisfactory and an unsuccessful experiment. The remaining system which the American states may adopt, is a union of them under one confederate republic. It will not be necessary to employ much time, or many arguments to shew, that this is the most eligible system that can be proposed. By adopting this system, the vigour and decision of a wide-spreading monarchy may be joined to the freedom and beneficence of a contracted republic. The extent of territory, the diversity of climate and soil, the number, and greatness, and connection of lakes and rives, with which the United States are interfected and almost surrounded, all indicate an enlarged government to be fit and advantageous for them. The principles and dispositions of their citizens, indicate that in this government, liberty shall reign triumphant. Such indeed have been the general opinions and wishes entertained since the æra of independence. If those opinions and wishes are as well-founded as they have been general, the late convention were juſtified in propoſing to their conſtituents, one confederate republic, as the beſt ſyſtem of a national government for the United States.

In forming this ſyſtem, it was proper to give minute attention to the intereſt of all the parts; but there was a duty of ſtill higher import—to feel and to ſhew a predominating regard to the ſuperior intereſts of the whole. If this great principle had not prevailed, the plan before us would never have made its appearance. The ſame principle that was ſo neceſſary in forming it, is equally neceſſary in our deliberations, whether we ſhould reject or ratify it.

I make theſe obſervations with a deſign to prove and illuſtrate this great and important truth—that in our deciſions on the work of the late convention, we ſhould not limit our views and regards to the ſtate of Pennſylvania. The aim of the convention was to form a ſyſtem of good and efficient government on the more extenſive ſcale of the United States. In this, and in every other inſtance, the work ſhould be judged with the ſame ſpirit, with which it was performed. A principle of duty as well as candour demands this.

We have remarked, that civil government is neceſſary to the perfection of ſociety: We now remark that civil liberty is neceſſary to the perfection of civil government. Civil liberty is natural liberty itſelf, diveſted only of that part, which, placed in the government, produces more good and happineſs to the community, than if it had remained in the individual. Hence it follows, that civil liberty, while it reſigns a part of natural liberty, retains the free and generous exerciſe of all the human faculties, ſo far as it is compatible with the public welfare.

In conſidering and developing the nature and end of the ſyſtem before us, it is neceſſary to mention another kind of liberty, which has not yet, as far as I know, received a name. I ſhall diſtinguiſh it by the appellation of *fœderal liberty*. When a ſingle government is inſtituted, the individuals, of which it is compoſed, ſurrender to it a part of their natural independence, which they before enjoyed as men. When a confederate republic is inſtituted, the commmunities, of which it is compoſed, ſurrender to it a part of their political independence, which they before enjoyed as ſtates. The principles, which directed, in the former caſe, what part of the natural liberty of the man ought to be given up, and what part ought to be retained, will give ſimilar directions in the latter caſe. The ſtates ſhould reſign, to the national government, that part, and that part only, of their political liberty, which placed in that government, will produce more good to the whole, than if it had remained in the several ſtates. While they reſign this part of their political liberty, they retain the free and generous exerciſe of all their other faculties as ſtates, ſo far as it is compatible with the welfare of the general and ſuperintending confederacy.

Since *ſtates* as well as *citizens* are repreſented in the conſtitution before us, and form the objects on which that conſtitution is propoſed to operate, it was neceſſary to notice and define *fœderal* as well as *civil* liberty.

Theſe general reflections have been made, in order to introduce, with more propriety and advantage, a practical illuſtration of the end propoſed to be accompliſhed by the late convention.

It has been too well known—it has been too ſeverely felt—that the preſent confederation is inadequate to the government and to the exigencies of the United States. The great ſtruggle for liberty in this country, ſhould it be unſucceſsful, will probably be the laſt one which ſhe will have for her exiſtence and proſperity, in any part of the globe. And it muſt be confeſſed, that this ſtruggle has, in ſome of the ſtages of its progreſs, been attended with ſymptoms, that foreboded no fortunate iſſue. To the iron hand of tyranny, which was lifted up againſt her, ſhe manifeſted, indeed, an intrepid ſuperiority. She broke in pieces the fetters, which were forged for her, and ſhewed, that ſhe was unaſſailable by force. But ſhe was environed with dangers of another kind, and ſpringing from a very different ſource. While ſhe kept her eye ſteadily fixed on the efforts of oppreſſion, licentiouſneſs was ſecretly undermining the rock on which ſhe ſtood.

Need I call to your remembrance the *contraſted* ſcenes, of which we have been witneſſes? On the glorious concluſion of our conflict with Britain, what high expectations were formed concerning us by others! what high expectations did we form concerning ourſelves! Have thoſe expectations been realized?—no. What has been the cauſe? Did our citizens loſe their perſeverance and magnanimity?—no. Did they become inſenſible of reſentment and indignation at any highhanded attempt, that might have been made to injure or enſlave them?—no. What then has been the cauſe? The truth is, we dreaded danger only on one ſide: This we manfully repelled. But on another ſide, danger, not leſs formidable, but more inſidious, ſtole in upon us; and our unſuſpicious tempers were not sufficiently attentive, either to its approach or to its operations. Those, whom foreign strength could not overpower, have well nigh become the victims of internal anarchy.

If we become a little more particular, we shall find that the foregoing representation is by no means exaggerated. When we had baffled all the menaces of foreign power, we neglected to establish among ourselves a government, that would ensure domestic vigour and stability. What was the consequence? The commencement of peace was the commencement of every disgrace and distress, that could befal a people in a peaceful state. Devoid of national power, we could not prohibit the extravagance of our importations, nor could we derive a revenue from their excess. Devoid of national importance, we could not procure, for our exports, a tolerable sale at foreign markets. Devoid of national credit, we saw our public securities melt in the hands of the holders, like snow before the sun. Devoid of national dignity, we could not, in some instances, perform our treaties, on our parts; and, in other instances, we could neither obtain nor compel the performance of them on the part of others. Devoid of national energy, we could not carry into execution our own resolutions, decisions or laws.

Shall I become more particular still? The tedious detail would disgust me: Nor is it now necessary. The years of languor are passed---We have felt the dishonor, with which we have been covered: We have seen the destruction, with which we have been threatened. We have penetrated to the causes of both, and when we have once discovered them, we have begun to search for the means of removing them. For the confirmation of these remarks, I need not appeal to an enumeration of facts. The proceedings of congress, and of the several states, are replete with them. They all point out the weakness and insufficiency as the cause, and an *efficient* general government as the only cure of our political distempers.

Under these impressions, and with these views, was the late convention appointed; and under these impressions, and with these views, the late convention met.

We now see the great end which they propose to accomplish. It was to frame, for the consideration of their constituents, one fœderal and national constitution—a constitution, that would produce the advantages of good, and prevent the inconveniences of bad government---a constitution, whose beneficence and energy would pervade the whole union; and bind and embrace the interests of every part---a constitution, that would ensure peace, freedom and happiness, to the states and people of America.

We are now naturally led to examine the means, by which they proposed to accomplish this end. This opens more particularly to our view the important discussion before us. But previously to our entering upon it, it will not be improper to state some general and leading principles of government, which will receive particular applications in the course of our investigations.

There necessarily exists in every government a power, from which there is no appeal; and which, for that reason, may be termed supreme, absolute and uncontrollable. Where does this power reside? To this question, writers on different governments will give different answers. Sir William Blackstone will tell you, that in Britain, the power is lodged in the British parliament, that the parliament may alter the form of the government; and that its power is absolute without control. The idea of a constitution, limiting and superintending the operations of legislative authority, seems not to have been accurately understood in Britain. There are, at least, no traces of practice, conformable to such a principle. The British constitution is just what the British parliament pleases. When the parliament transferred legislative authority to Henry VIII. the act transferring could not in the strict acceptation of the term, be called unconstitutional.

To control the power and conduct of the legislature by an over-ruling constitution, was an improvement in the science and practice of government, reserved to the American states.

Perhaps some politician, who has not considered, with sufficient accuracy, our political systems, would answer, that in our governments, the supreme power was vested in the constitutions. This opinion approaches a step nearer to the truth; but does not reach it. The truth is, that, in our governments, the supreme, absolute and uncontrolable power *remains* in the people. As our constitutions are superior to our legislatures; so the people are superior to our constitutions. Indeed the superiority, in this last instance, is much greater; for the people possess, over our constitutions, control in *act*, as well as in right.

THE CONVENTION.

The confequence is, that the people may change the ſtitutions, whenever, and however they pleaſe. This right, of which no poſitive inſtitution can ever deprive t

Theſe important truths, ſir, are far from being m ſpeculative: We, at this moment, ſpeak and deliberat der their immediate and benign influence. To the oper of theſe truths, we are to aſcribe the ſcene, hitherto ı rallelled, which America now exhibits to the world---a tle, a peaceful, a voluntary and a deliberate tranſition one conſtitution of government to another. In other of the world, the idea of revolutions in government is, mournful and an indiſſoluble aſſociation, connected witl idea of wars, and all the calamities attendant on wars. happy experience teaches us to view ſuch revolutions i very different light—to conſider them only as progr ſteps in improving the knowledge of government, an creaſing the happineſs of ſociety and mankind.

Oft have I viewed, with ſilent pleaſure and admir: the force and prevalence, through the United States the ſupreme power reſides in the people; and that never part with it. It may be called the *Panacea* in tics. There can be no diſordet in the community bu here receive a radical cure. If the error be in the le ture, it may be corrected by the conſtitution: If in th ſtitution, it may be corrected by the people. There remedy, therefore, for every diſtemper in governmen the people are not wanting to themſelves. For a p wanting to themſelves, there is no remedy: From power, as we have ſeen, there is no appeal: To thei ror, there is no ſuperior principle of correction.

There are three ſimple ſpecies of government---Mona where the ſupreme power is in a ſingle perſon.----Ariſı cy, where the ſupreme power is in a ſelect aſſembly members of which either fill up, by election, the vaca in their own body; or ſucceed to their places in it by inherit property, or in reſpect of ſome *perſonal* right or quali on---a Republic or Democracy, where the people at *retain* the ſupreme power, and act either collectively (repreſentation.

Each of theſe ſpecies of government has its advan and diſadvantages.

The advantages of a monarchy are ſtrength, diſ[ſecrecy, unity of counſel. Its diſadvantages are---Tyr expense, ignorance of the situation and wants of the people, insecurity, unnecessary wars, evils attending elections or successions.

The advantages of aristocracy are---Wisdom, arising from experience and education. Its disadvantages are---Dissentions among themselves, oppression to the lower orders.

The advantages of democracy are---Liberty, equal, cautious and salutary laws, public spirit, frugality, peace, opportunities of exciting and producing abilities of the best citizens. Its disadvantages are dissentions, the delay and disclosure of public counsels, the imbecility of public measures retarded by the necessity of a numerous consent.

A government may be composed of two or more of the simple forms above-mentioned. Such is the British government. It would be an improper government for the United States; because it is inadequate to such an extent of teritory; and because it is suited to an establishment of different orders of men. A more minute comparison between some parts of the British constitution, and some parts of the plan before us, may perhaps find a proper place in a subsequent period of our business.

What is the nature and kind of that government, which has been proposed for the United States, by the late convention? In its principle, it is purely democratical: But that principle is applied in different forms, in order to obtain the advantages, and exclude the inconveniencies of the simple modes of government.

If we take an extended and accurate view of it, we shall find the streams of power running in different directions, in different dimensions, and at different heights, watering, adorning and fertilizing the fields and meadows, thro' which their courses are led; but if we trace them, we shall discover, that they all originally flow from one abundant fountain.

In THIS CONSTITUTION, *all authority is derived from the* PEOPLE.

Fit occasions will hereafter offer for particular remarks on the different parts of the plan. I have now to ask pardon of the house for detaining them so long.

WEDNESDAY, OCTOBER 28, 1787, A. M.
Mr. WILSON.

This will be a proper time for making an observation or two, on what may be called the preamble to this constitution. I had occasion, on a former day, to mention that t[he] leading principle in politics, and that which pervades t[he] American constitutions, is, that the supreme power resides [in] the people; this constitution, Mr. President, opens wit[h a] solemn and practical recognition of that principle; "W[E] THE PEOPLE OF THE UNITED STATES, " order to form a more perfect union, establish justice, [&c.] " DO ORDAIN AND ESTABLISH this constituti[on] " for the United States of America." It is announced [in] their name, it receives its political existence from their [au]thority—they ordain and establish: What is the necess[ary] consequence?—those who ordain and establish, have [the] power, if they think proper, to repeal and annul.—A p[ro]per attention to this principle may, perhaps, give ease to [the] minds of some, who have heard much concerning the nec[es]sity of a bill of rights.

Its establishment, I apprehend, has more force, tha[n a] volume written on the subject—it renders this truth evide[nt,] that the people have a right to do what they please, w[ith] regard to the government. I confess, I feel a kind [of] pride, in considering the striking difference between [the] foundation, on which the liberties of this country are [de]clared to stand in this constitution, and the footing on wh[ich] the liberties of England are said to be placed. The ma[gna] charta of England is an instrument of high value to [the] people of that country. But, Mr. President, from w[hat] source does that instrument derive the liberties of the in[ha]bitants of that kingdom?—Let it speak for itself.—The k[ing] says, " *we* have *given* and *granted* to all archbishops, bish[ops,] " abbots, priors, earls, barons, and to all the freemer[of] " this our realm, these liberties following, to be kept in [our] " kingdom of England for ever." When this was assu[med] as the leading principle of that government, it was no w[on]der that the people were anxious to obtain bills of rig[hts,] and to take every opportunity of enlarging and secu[ring] their liberties. But, here, Sir, the fee-simple remain[s in] the people at large, and, by this constitution, they do [not] part with it.

Mr. WILSON.

I am called upon to give a reason, why the conver[ntion] omitted to add a bill of rights to the work before you[.—I] confess, Sir, I did think that in point of propriety, the

F

nourable gentleman ought firſt to have furniſhed ſome reaſons, to ſhew ſuch an addition to be neceſſary; it is natural to prove the affirmative of a propoſition; and if he had eſtabliſhed the propriety of this addition, he might then have aſked, why it was not made.

I cannot ſay, Mr. Preſident, what were the reaſons, of every member of that convention, for not adding a bill of rights; I believe the truth is, that ſuch an idea never entered the mind of many of them. I don't recollect to have heard the ſubject mentioned, till within about three days of the time of our riſing, and even then there was no direct motion offered for any thing of this kind.---I may be miſtaken in this; but as far as my memory ſerves me, I believe it was the caſe. A propoſition to adopt a meaſure, that would have ſuppoſed that we were throwing into the general government, every power not expreſsly reſerved by the people, would have been ſpurned at, in that houſe, with the greateſt indignation; even in a ſingle government, if the powers of the people reſt on the ſame eſtabliſhment, as is expreſſed in this conſtitution, a bill of rights is by no means a neceſſary meaſure. In a government poſſeſſed of enumerated powers, ſuch a meaſure would be not only unneceſſary, but prepoſterous and dangerous: whence comes this notion, that in the United States there is no ſecurity without a bill of rights? Have the citizens of South-Carolina no ſecurity for their liberties? they have no bill of rights. Are the citizens on the eaſtern ſide of the Delaware leſs free, or leſs ſecured in their liberties, than thoſe on the weſtern ſide? The ſtate of New-Jerſey has no bill of rights. ---The ſtate of New-York has no bill of rights.---The ſtates of Connecticut and Rhode-Iſland have no bills of rights.--- I know not whether I have exactly enumerated the ſtates who have thought it unneceſſary to add a bill of rights to their conſtitutions; but this enumeration, Sir, will ſerve to ſhew by experience, as well as principle, that even in ſingle governments, a bill of rights is not an eſſential or neceſſary meaſure.---But in a government, conſiſting of enumerated powers, ſuch as is propoſed for the United States, a bill of rights would not only be unneceſſary, but, in my humble judgment, highly imprudent. In all ſocieties, there are many powers and rights, which cannot be particularly enumerated. A bill of rights annexed to a conſtitution, is an enumeration of the powers reſerved. If we attempt an enumeration, every thing that is not enumerated, is presumed to be given. The consequence is, that an imperfect enumeration would throw all implied power into the scale of the government; and the rights of the people would be rendered incomplete. On the other hand; an imperfect enumeration of the powers of government, reserves all implied power to the people; and, by that means the constitution becomes incomplete; but of the two it is much safer to run the risk on the side of the constitution; for an omission in the enumeration of the powers of government, is neither so dangerous, nor important, as an omission in the enumeration of the rights of the people.

Mr. President, as we are drawn into this subject, I beg leave to pursue its history a little further. The doctrine and practice of declarations of rights have been borrowed from the conduct of the people of England, on some remarkable occasions; but the principles and maxims, on which their government is constituted, are widely different from those of ours. I have already stated the language of magna charta. After repeated confirmations of that instrument, and after violations of it, repeated equally often, the next step taken in this business, was, when the petition of rights was presented to Charles the first.

It concludes in this manner, " all of which they most humbly *pray* to be allowed, as their rights and liberties, according to the laws and statutes of this realm. * One of the most material statutes of the realm was magna charta; so that we find they continue upon the old ground, as to the foundation on which they rest their liberties. It was not till the æra of the revolution, that the two houses assume an higher tone, and " *demand* and insist upon all the premises " as their undoubted rights and liberties." † But when the whole transaction is considered, we shall find that those rights, and liberties, are claimed only on the foundation of an original contract, supposed to have been made at some former period, between the king and the people. ‡

But, in this constitution, the citizens of the United States appear dispensing a part of their original power, in what manner and what proportion they think fit. They never

---

* 8th Parl. Hist. 150.
† 2 Par. Deb. 261.
‡ 1 Blackstone, 233.

part with the whole; and they retain the right of re-calling what they part with. When, therefore, they poffefs, as I have already mentioned, the fee-fimple of authority, why fhould they have recourfe to the minute and fubordinate remedies, which can be neceffary only to thofe, who pafs the fee, and referve only a rent-charge?

To every fuggeftion concerning a bill of rights, the citizens of the United States may always fay, WE referve the right to do what we pleafe.

Mr. WILSON.

I concur moft fincerely, with the honorable gentleman who was laft up, in one fentiment, that if our liberties will be infecure under this fyftem of government, it will become our duty not to adopt, but to reject it. On the contrary, if it will fecure the liberties of the citizens of America, if it will not only fecure their liberties, but procure them happinefs, it becomes our duty, on the other hand, to affent to and ratify it. With a view to conduct us fafely, and gradually, to the determination of that important queftion, I fhall beg leave, to notice fome of the objections, that have fallen from the hon. gentleman from Cumberland (Whitehill.) But, before I proceed, permit me to make one general remark. Liberty has a formidable enemy on each hand; on one, there is tyranny, on the other licentioufnefs: in order to guard againft the latter, proper powers ought to be given to government: in order to guard againft the former, thofe powers ought to be properly diftributed. It has been mentioned, and attempts have been made to eftablifh the pofition, that the adoption of this conftitution will neceffarily be followed by the annihilation of all the ftate governments. If this was a neceffary confequence, the objection would operate in my mind with exceeding great force. But, fir, I think the inference is rather unnatural, that a government will produce the annihilation of others, upon the very exiftence of which its own exiftence depends. Let us, fir, examine this conftitution, and mark its proportions, and arrangements. It is compofed of three great conftituent parts, the legiflative department, the executive department, and the judicial department. The legiflative department is fubdivided into two branches, the houfe of reprefentatives and the fenate. Can there be a houfe of reprefentatives, in the general go-

vernment, after the state governments are annihilated?----
Care is taken to express the character of the electors in such a manner, that even the popular branch of the general government, cannot exist, unless the governments of the states continue in existence.

How do I prove this? By the regulation that is made, concerning the important subject of giving suffrage. Article the first, section second, " and the electors in each state, shall have the qualifications for electors of the most numerous branch of the state legislature." Now, Sir, in order to know who are qualified to be electors of the house of representatives, we are to enquire, who are qualified to be electors of the legislature of each state; if there be no legislatures in the states, there can be no electors of them: if there be no such electors, there is a criterion to know who are qualified to elect members of the house of representatives. By this short, plain deduction, the existence of state legislatures, is proved to be essential to the existence of the general government.

Let us proceed now to the second branch of the legislative department. In the system before you, the senators, Sir, those tyrants that are to devour the legislatures of the states, are to be chosen by the state legislatures themselves. Need any thing more be said on this subject? So far is the principle of each state's retaining the power of self-preservation, from being weakened or endangered by the general government, that the convention went further, perhaps, than was strictly proper, in order to secure it; for in this second branch of the legislature, each state, without regard to its importance, is entitled to an equal vote. And in the articles, respecting amendments of this constitution, it is provided " that no " state, without its consent, shall be deprived of its equal " suffrage in the senate."

Does it appear then, that provision for the continuance of the state governments was neglected, in framing this constitution? On the contrary, it was a favorite object in the convention to secure them.

The president of the United States, is to be chosen by electors appointed in the different states, in such manner as the legislature shall direct. Unless there be legislatures to appoint electors, the president cannot be chosen; the idea, therefore, of the existing government of the states, is presupposed in the very mode of constituting the legislative and

the executive departments of the general government.---
The same principle will apply to the judicial department.
The judges are to be nominated by the president, and appointed by him, with the advice and consent of the senate.
This shews, that the judges cannot exist without the president and senate. I have already shewn that the president and senate cannot exist without the existence of the state legislatures. Have I mistated any thing? Is not the evidence indisputable, that the state governments will be preserved, or that the general government must tumble amidst their ruins? It is true, indeed, Sir, although it presupposes the existence of state governments, yet this constitution does not suppose them to be the sole power to be respected.

In the articles of confederation the people are unknown, but in this plan they are represented: and in one of the branches of the legislature they are represented, immediately, by persons of their own choice.

I hope these observations, on the nature and formation of this system, are seen in their full force; many of them were so seen by some gentlemen of the late convention. After all this, could it have been expected, that assertions, such as have been hazarded on this floor, would have been made, "that it was the business of their deliberations, to destroy "the state governments, that they employed four months "to accomplish this object, and that such was their inten-"tions?" That honorable gentleman may be better qualified to judge of their intentions than themselves. I know my own, and, as to those of the other members I believe, that they have been very improperly and unwarrantably represented; intended to destroy! where did *he* obtain his information? Let the tree be judged of by its fruit.

Mr. President, the only proof that is attempted to be drawn from the work itself, is that which has been urged from the fourth section of the first article. I will read it, " The times, places and manner of holding elections, for senators and representatives, shall be prescribed in each state by the legislature thereof; but the congress may at any time, by law make or alter such regulations, except as to the places of chusing senators."

And is this a proof, that it was intended to carry on this government, after the state government should be dissolved and abrogated? This clause is not only a proper, but a necessary one. I have already shewn what pains have been taken in the convention to fecure the prefervation of the ftate governments. I hope, Sir, that it was no crime, to fow the feed of felf-prefervation in the fœderal government; without this claufe it would not poffefs felf-preferving power. By this claufe the times, places and manner of holding elections, fhall be prefcribed in each ftate, by the legiflature thereof. I think it highly proper that the fœderal government fhould throw the exercife of this power into the hands of the ftate legiflatures; but not that it fhould be placed there entirely without control.

If the congrefs had it not in their power to make regulations, what might be the confequences? Some ftates might make no regulations at all on the fubject. And fhall the exiftence of the houfe of reprefentatives, the immediate reprefentation of the people in congrefs, depend upon the will and pleafure of the ftate governments? Another thing may poffibly happen, I don't fay it will; but we were obliged to guard even againft poffibilities, as well as probabilities. A legiflature may be willing to make the neceffary regulations, yet the minority of that legiflature may, by abfenting themfelves, break up the houfe, and prevent the execution of the intention of the majority. I have fuppofed the cafe, that fome ftate governments may make no regulations at all; it is poffible alfo that they may make improper regulations. I have heard it furmifed by the opponents of this conftitution, that the congrefs may order the election for Pennfylvania to be held at Pittfburg, and thence conclude, that it would be improper for them to have the exercife of the power; but fuppofe on the other hand, that the affembly fhould order an election to be held at Pittfburg, ought not the general government to have the power to alter fuch improper election of one of its own conftituent parts? But there is an additional reafon ftill, that fhews the neceffity of this provifionary claufe. The members of the fenate are elected by the ftate legiflatures. If thofe legiflatures poffeffed, uncontrolled, the power of prefcribing the times, places and manner of electing members of the houfe of reprefentatives, the members of one branch of the general legiflature would be the tenants at will of the electors of the other branch; and the general government would lie proftrate at the mercy of the legiflatures of the feveral ftates.

I will afk now, is the inference fairly drawn, that the general government was intended to fwallow up the ftate governments? or was it calculated to anfwer fuch end? or do its framers deferve fuch cenfure from honorable gentlemen? We find on examining this paragraph, that it contains nothing more, than the maxims of felf-prefervation, fo abundantly fecured by this conftitution to the individual ftates. Several other objections have been mentioned; I will not, at this time, enter into a difcuffion of them, though I may hereafter take notice of fuch as have any fhew of weight. But I thought it neceffary to offer at this time, the obfervations I have made; becaufe I confider this as an important fubject; and think the objection would be a ftrong one, if it was well founded.

Friday, November 30, 1787, A. M

Mr. Wilson.

It is objected that the number of members in the houfe of reprefentatives is too fmall. This is a fubject fomething embarraffing, and the convention who framed the article, felt the embarraffment. Take either fide of the queftion, and you are neceffarily led into difficulties. A large reprefentation, fir, draws along with it a great expence. We all know that expence is offered as an objection to this fyftem of government, and certainly had the reprefentation been greater, the clamour would have been on that fide, and perhaps, with fome degree of juftice. But the expence is not the fole objection; it is the opinion of fome writers, that a deliberative body ought not to confift of more than one hundred members. I think, however, that there might be fafety and propriety in going beyond that number; but certainly there is fome number fo large, that it would be improper to encreafe them beyond it. The Britifh houfe of commons confifts of upwards of five hundred. The fenate of Rome confifted, it is faid, at fome times, of one thoufand members. This laft number is certainly too great.

The convention endeavoured to fteer a middle courfe, and when we confider the fcale on which they formed their calculation, there are ftrong reafons, why the reprefentation fhould not have been larger. On the ratio that they have fixed, of one for every thirty-thoufand, and according to the generally received opinion of the increase of population throughout the United States, the present number of their inhabitants will be doubled in twenty five years, and according to that progressive proportion, and the ratio of one member for thirty thousand inhabitants, the house of representatives will, within a single century, consist of more than six hundred members; permit me to add a further observation on the numbers—that a large number is not so necessary in this case, as in the cases of state legislatures. In them there ought to be a representation sufficient to declare the situation of every county, town and district; and if of every individual, so much the better, because their legislative powers extend to the particular interest and convenience of each, but in the general government, its objects are enumerated, and are not confined in their causes or operations, to a county, or even to a single state.—No one power is of such a nature, as to require the minute knowledge of situations and circumstances necessary in state governments, possessed of general legislative authority; these were the reasons, sir, that I believe had influence on the convention to agree to the number of thirty thousand, and when the inconveniencies and conveniencies on both sides are compared, it would be difficult to say what would be a number more unexceptionable.

SATURDAY, DECEMBER 1, 1787, A. M.

Mr. WILSON.

The secret is now disclosed, and it is discovered to be a dread, that the boasted state sovereignties, will under this system be disrobed of part of their power. Before I go into the examination of this point, let me ask one important question---Upon what principle is it contended that the sovereign power resides in the state governments? the honorable gentleman has said truly, that there can be no subordinate sovereignty. Now if there can not, my position is, that the sovereignty resides in the people, they have not parted with it; they have only dispensed such portions of power as were conceived necessary for the public welfare. This constitution stands upon this broad principle. I know very well, sir, that the people have hitherto been shut out of the federal government, but it is not meant that they should any longer be dispossessed of their rights. In order to recognize this leading principle, the propofed fyftem fets out with a declaration, that its exiftence depends upon the fupreme authority of the people alone. We have heard much about a confolidated government.---I wifh the honorable gentleman would condefcend to give us a definition of what he meant by it. I think this the more neceffary, becaufe I apprehend that the term, in the numerous times it has been ufed, has not always been ufed in the fame fenfe. It may be faid and I believe it has been faid, that a confolidated government is fuch, as will abforb and deftroy the governments of the feveral ftates. If it is taken in this view, the plan before us is not a confolidated government, as I fhewed on a former day, and may, if neceffary, fhew further on fome future occafion.—On the other hand, if it is meant, that the general government will take from the ftate governments their power in fome particulars, it is confeffed and evident, that this will be its operation and effect.

When the principle is once fettled, that the people are the fource of authority, the confequence is, that they may take from the fubordinate governments powers with which they have hitherto trufted them, and place thofe powers in the general government, if it is thought that there they will be productive of more good.—They can diftribute one portion of power, to the more contracted circle, called ftate governments : they can alfo furnifh another proportion to the government of the United States. Who will undertake to fay, as a ftate officer, that the people may not give to the general government what powers, and for what purpofes they pleafe ? how comes it, fir, that thefe ftate governments dictate to their fuperiors ? to the majefty of the people ? When I fay the majefty of the people, I mean the thing and not a mere compliment to them. The honorable gentleman went a ftep further and faid, that the ftate governments were kept out of this government altogether. The truth is, and it is a leading principle in this fyftem, that not the ftates only, but the people alfo fhall be here reprefented. And if this is a crime, I confefs the general government is chargeable with it ; but I have no idea, that a fafe fyftem of power, in the government, fufficient to manage the general intereft of the United States, could be drawn from any other fcource, or refted in any other authority than that of the people at large, and I confider this authority as the rock on which this ftructure will ftand.—If this principle is unfounded, the system must fall. If honorable gentlemen, before they undertake to oppose this principle, will shew that the people have parted with their power to the state governments, then I confess I cannot support this constitution. It is asked can there be two taxing powers? Will the people submit to two taxing powers? I think they will, when the taxes are required for the public welfare, by persons appointed immediately by their fellow citizens.

But I believe this doctrine is a very disagreeable one to some of the state governments. All the objects that will furnish an encrease of revenue, are eagerly seised by them; perhaps this will lead to the reason why a state government, when she was obliged to pay only about an eighth part of the loan-office certificates, should voluntarily undertake the payment of about one-third part of them. This power of taxation will be regulated in the general government upon equitable principles. No state can have more than her just proportion to discharge—no longer will government be obliged to assign her funds for the payment of debts she does not owe. Another objection has been taken, that the judicial powers are coextensive with the objects of the national government. So far as I can understand the idea of magistracy in every government, this seems to be a proper arrangement; the judicial department is considered as a part of the executive authority of government. Now, I have no idea that the authority should be restrained, so as not to be able to perform its functions with full effect. I would not have the legislature fit to make laws, which cannot be executed. It is not meant here that the laws shall be a dead letter; it is meant, that they shall be carefully and duly considered, before they are enacted; and that then they shall be honestly and faithfully executed. This observation naturally leads to a more particular consideration of the government before us. In order, sir, to give permanency, stability and security to any government, I conceive it of essential importance, that its legislature should be restrained; that there should not only be, what we call a *passive*, but an *active* power over it; for of all kinds of despotism, this is the most dreadful, and the most difficult to be corrected. With how much contempt have we seen the authority of the people, treated by the legislature of this state—and how often have we seen it making laws in one session, that have been repealed the next, either on account of the fluctuation of party, or their own impropriety.

This could not have been the cafe in a compound legiflature; it is therefore proper to have efficient reftraints upon the legiflative body. Thefe reftraints arife from different fources: I will mention fome of them. In this conftitution they will be produced in a very confiderable degree, by a divifion of the power in the legiflative body itfelf. Under this fyftem, they may arife likewife from the interference of thofe officers, who will be introduced into the executive and judicial departments. They may fpring alfo from another fource; the election by the people; and finally, under this conftitution, they may proceed from the great and laft refort—from the PEOPLE themfelves. I fay, under this conftitution, the legiflature may be reftrained, and kept within its prefcribed bounds, by the interpofition of the judicial department. This I hope, fir, to explain clearly and fatisfactorily. I had occafion, on a former day, to ftate that the power of the conftitution was paramount to the power of the legiflature, acting under that conftitution. For it is poffible that the legiflature, when acting in that capacity, may tranfgrefs the bounds affigned to it, and an act may pafs, in the ufual *mode*, notwithftanding that trangreffion; but when it comes to be difcuffed before the judges—when they confider its principles, and find it to be incompatible with the fuperior power of the conftitution, it is their duty to pronounce it void; and judges independent, and not obliged to look to every feffion, for a continuance of their falaries, will behave with intrepidity, and refufe to the act the fanction of judicial authority. In the fame manner, the prefident of the United States could fhield himfelf, and refufe to carry into effect, an act that violates the conftitution.

In order to fecure the prefident from any dependence upon the legiflature, as to his falary, it is provided, that he fhall, at ftated times, receive for his fervices, a compenfation that fhall neither be encreafed nor diminifhed, during the period for which he fhall have been elected, and that he fhall not receive, within that period, any other emolument from the United States, or any of them.

To fecure to the judges this independence, it is ordered that they fhall receive for their fervices, a compenfation which fhall not be diminifhed during their continuance in office. The congrefs may be reftrained, by the election of its conftituent parts. If a legiflature fhall make a law contrary to the conftitution, or oppreffive to the people, they have it in their power, every second year, in one branch, and every sixth year in the other, to displace the men, who act thus inconsistent with their duty; and if this is not sufficient, they have still a further power; they may assume into their own hands, the alteration of the constitution itself—they may revoke the lease, when the conditions are broken by the tenant. But the most useful restraint upon the legislature, because it operates constantly, arises from the division of its power, among two branches, and from the qualified negative of the president upon both. As this government is formed, there are two sources from which the representation is drawn, though they both ultimately flow from the people. *States now exist and others will come into existence*; it was thought proper that they should be represented in the general government. But, gentlemen will please to remember, this constitution was not framed merely for the states; it was framed for the PEOPLE also; and the popular branch of the congress, will be the objects of their immediate choice.

The two branches will serve as checks upon each other; they have the same legislative authorities, except in one instance. Money bills must originate in the house of representatives. The senate can pass no law without the concurrence of the house of representatives; nor can the house of representatives, without the concurrence of the senate. I believe, sir, that the observation which I am now going to make, will apply to mankind in every situation; they will act with more caution, and perhaps more integrity, if their proceedings are to be under the inspection and control of another, than when they are not. From this principle, the proceedings of congress will be conducted with a degree of circumspection not common in single bodies, where nothing more is necessary to be done, than to carry the business through amongst themselves, whether it be right or wrong. In compound legislatures, every object must be submitted to a distinct body, not influenced by the arguments, or warped by the prejudices of the other. And, I believe, that the persons who will form the congress, will be cautious in running the risk, *with a bare majority*, of having the negative of the president put on their proceedings. As there will be more circumspection in forming the laws, so there will be more stability in the laws when made. Indeed one is the consequence of the other; for what has been well considered, and founded in good sense, will, in practice, be useful and salutary, and of consequence will not   to be soon repealed. Though two bomay not possess more wisdom or patriotism, than what may be found in a single body, yet they will necessarily introduce a greater degree of precision. An indigested and inaccurate code of laws, is one of the most dangerous things that can be introduced into any government. The force of this observation is well known by every gentleman that has attended to the laws of this state. This, sir, is a very important advantage, that will arise from this division of the legislative authority.

I will proceed now to take some notice of a still further restraint upon the legislature---I mean the qualified negative of the president. I think this will be attended with very important advantages, for the security and happiness of the people of the United States. The president, sir, will not be a stranger to our country, to our laws, or to our wishes. He will, under this constitution, be placed in office as the president of the whole union, and will be chosen in such a manner that he may be justly stiled THE MAN OF THE PEOPLE; being elected by the different parts of the United States, he will consider himself as not particularly interested for any one of them, but will watch over the whole with paternal care and affection. This will be the natural conduct to recommend himself to those who placed him in that high chair, and I consider it as a very important advantage, that such a man must have every law presented to him, before it can become binding upon the United States. He will have before him the fullest information of our situation, he will avail himself not only of records and official communications, foreign and domestic, but he will have also the advice of the executive officers in the different departments of the general government.

If in consequence of this information and advice, he exercise the authority given to him, the effect will not be lost—he returns his objections, together with the bill, and unless two thirds of both branches of the legislature are *now* found to approve it, it does not become a law. But even if his objections do not prevent its passing into a law, they will not be useless; they will be kept together with the law, and, in the archives of congress, will be valuable and practical materials, to form the minds of posterity for legislation—if it is found that the law operates inconveniently, or oppressively, the people may discover in the president's objections, the source of that inconvenience or oppression. Further, sir, when objections shall have been made, it is provided, in order to secure the greatest degree of caution and reponsibility, that the votes of both houses shall be determined by yeas and nays, and the names of the persons, voting for and against the bill, shall be entered in the journal of each house respectively. Thus much I have thought proper to say, with regard to the distribution of the legislative authority, and the restraints under which it will be exercised.

The gentleman in opposition strongly insists, that the general clause at the end of the eighth section, gives to congress a power of legislating generally ; but I cannot conceive by what means he will render the word susceptible of that expansion. Can the words, the congress shall have power to make all laws, which shall be necessary and proper to carry into execution the foregoing powers, be capable of giving them general legislative power?—I hope that it is not meant to give to congress merely an illusive shew of authority, to deceive themselves or constituents any longer. On the contrary, I trust it is meant, that they shall have the power of carrying into effect the laws, which they shall make under the powers vested in them by this constitution. In answer to the gentleman from Fayette (Mr. Smilie,) on the subject of the press, I beg leave to make an observation ; it is very true, sir, that this constitution says nothing with regard to that subject, nor was it necessary, because it will be found, that there is given to the general government no power whatsoever concerning it ; and no law in pursuance of the constitution, can possibly be enacted, to destroy that liberty.

I heard the honorable gentleman make this general assertion, that the Congress was certainly vested with power to make such a law, but I would be glad to know by what part of this constitution such a power is given? Until that is done, I shall not enter into a minute investigation of the matter, but shall at present satisfy myself with giving an answer to a question that has been put. It has been asked, if a law should be made to punish libels, and the judges should proceed under that law, what chance would the printer have of an acquittal? And it has been said he would drop into a den of devouring monsters.

I presume it was not in the view of the honorable gentleman to say there is no such thing as a libel, or that the writers of such ought not to be punished. The idea of the liberty of the press, is not carried so far as this in any country—

what is meant by the liberty of the prefs is, that there fhould be no antecedent reftraint upon it; but that every author is refponfible when he attacks the fecurity or welfare of the government, or the fafety, character and property of the individual.

With regard to attacks upon the public, the mode of proceeding is by a profecution. Now if a libel is written, it muft be within fome one of the United States, or the diftrict of congrefs. With regard to that diftrict, I hope it will take care to preferve this as well as the other rights of freemen; for whatever diftrict congrefs may chufe, the ceffion of it cannot be completed without the confent of its inhabitants. Now fir, if this libel is to be tried, it muft be tried where the offence was committed; for under this conftitution, as declared in the fecond fection of the third article, the trial muft be held in the ftate; thereforeon this occafion it muft be tried where it was publifhed, if the indictment is for publifhing; and it muft be tried likewife by a jury of that ftate. Now I would afk, is the perfon profecuted in a worfe fituation under the general government, even if it had the power to make laws on this fubject, than he is at prefent under the ftate government? It is true, there is no particular regulation made, to have the jury come from the body of the county in which the offence was committed; but there are fome ftates in which this mode of collecting juries is contrary to their eftablifhed cuftom, and gentlemen ought to confider that this conftitution was not meant merely for Pennfylvania. In fome ftates the juries are not taken from a fingle county. In Virginia, the fheriff, I believe, is not confined, even to the inhabitants of the ftate, but is at liberty to take any man he pleafes, and put him on the jury. In Maryland I think a fett of jurors ferve for the whole Weftern Shore, and another for the Eaftern Shore.

I beg to make one remark on what one gentleman has faid, with refpect to amendments being propofed to this conftitution. To whom are the cconvention to make report of fuch amendments? He tells you, to the prefent congrefs. I do not wifh to report to that body, the reprefentatives only of the ftate governments; they may not be difpofed to admit the people into a participation of their power. It has alfo been fuppofed, that a wonderful unanimity fubfifts among thofe who are enemies to the propofed fyftem. On this point I alfo differ from the gentleman who made the observation. I have taken every pains in my power, and read every publication I could meet with, in order to gain information; and as far as I have been able to judge, the opposition is inconsiderable and inconsistent. Instead of agreeing in their objections, those who make them, bring forward such as are diametrically opposite. On one hand, it is said, that the representation in congress is too small; on the other, it is said to be too numerous. Some think the authority of the senate too great; some that of the house of representatives; and some that of both. Others draw their fears from the powers of the president; and like the iron race of Cadmus, these opponents rise, only to destroy each other.

MONDAY, DECEMBER 3, 1787, A. M.

MR. WILSON.

Take detached parts of any system whatsoever, in the manner these gentlemen have hitherto taken this constitution, and you will make it absurd and inconsistent with itself. I do not confine this observation to human performances alone; it will apply to divine writings. An anecdote, which I have heard, exemplifies this observation: When Sternhold and Hopkin's version of the psalms was usually sung in churches, a line was first read by the clerk, and then sung by the congregation. A sailor had stepped in, and heard the clerk read this line:

"The Lord will come, and he will not—"

The sailor stared; and when the clerk read the next line,

"Keep silence; but speak out,"

the sailor left the church, thinking the people were not in their senses.

This story may convey an idea of the treatment of the plan before you; for although it contains sound sense, when connected, yet by the detached manner of considering it, it appears highly absurd.

MR. WILSON.

Much fault has been found with the mode of expression, used in the first clause of the ninth section of the first article. I believe I can assign a reason, why that mode of expression was used; and why the term slave was not directly admitted in this conſtitution ;—and as to the manner of laying taxes, this is not the firſt time that the ſubject has come into the view of the United States, and of the legiſlatures of the ſeveral ſtates. The gentleman (Mr. Findley) will recollect, that in the preſent congreſs, the quota of the fœderal debt, and general expences, was to be in proportion to the value of LAND, and other enumerated property, within the ſtates. After trying this for a number of years, it was found on all hands, to be a mode that could not be carried into execution. Congreſs were ſatisfied of this, and in the year 1783, recommended, in conformity with the powers they poſſeſs'd under the articles of confederation, that the quota ſhould be according to the number of free people, including thoſe bound to ſervitude, and excluding Indians not taxed. Theſe were the very expreſſions uſed in 1783, and the fate of this recommendation was ſimilar to all their other reſolutions. It was not carried into effect, but it was adopted by no fewer than eleven, out of thirteen ſtates; and it can not but be matter of ſurpriſe, to hear gentlemen, who agreed to this very mode of expreſſion at that time, come forward and ſtate it as an objection on the preſent occaſion. It was natural, ſir, for the late convention, to adopt the mode after it had been agreed to by eleven ſtates, and to uſe the expreſſion, which they found had been received as unexceptionable before. With reſpect to the clauſe, reſtricting congreſs from prohibiting the migration or importation of ſuch perſons, as any of the ſtates now exiſting, ſhall think proper to admit, prior to the year 1808. The honorable gentleman ſays, that this clauſe is not only dark, but intended to grant to congreſs, for that time, the power to admit the importation of ſlaves. No ſuch thing was intended; but I will tell you what was done, and it gives me high pleaſure, that ſo much was done. Under the preſent confederation, the ſtates may admit the importation of ſlaves as long as they pleaſe; but by this article after the year 1808, the congreſs will have power to prohibit ſuch importation, notwithſtanding the diſpoſitian of any ſtate to the contrary. I conſider this as laying the foundation for baniſhing ſlavery out of this country; and though the period is more diſtant than I could wiſh, yet it will produce the ſame kind, gradual change, which was purſued in Pennſylvania. It is with much ſatisfaction I view this power in the general government, whereby they may lay an interdiction on this reproachful trade; but an immediate advantage is also obtained, for a tax or duty may be imposed on such importation, not exceeding ten dollars for each person; and, this sir, operates as a partial prohibition; it was all that could be obtained, I am sorry it was no more; but from this I think there is reason to hope, that yet a few years, and it will be prohibited altogether; and in the mean time, the new states which are to be formed, will be under the control of congress in this particular; and slaves will never be introduced amongst them. The gentleman says, that it is unfortunate in another point of view; it means to prohibit the introduction of white people from Europe, as this tax may deter them from coming amongst us; a little impartiality and attention will discover the care that the convention took in selecting their language. The words are, the *migration or* IMPORTATION of such persons, &c. shall not be prohibited by congress prior to the year 1808, but a tax or duty may be imposed on such IMPORTATION; it is observable here, that the term migration is dropped, when a tax or duty is mentioned; so that congress have power to impose the tax, only on those imported.

TUESDAY DECEMBER, 4, 1787, A. M.

Mr. WILSON.

I shall take this opportunity, of giving an answer to the objections already urged against the constitution; I shall then point out some of those qualities, that entitle it to the attention and approbation of this convention; and after having done this, I shall take a fit opportunity of stating the consequences, which I apprehend will result from rejecting it, and those which will probably result from its adoption. I have given the utmost attention to the debates and the objections, that from time to time have been made by the three gentlemen who speak in opposition. I have reduced them to some order, perhaps not better than that in which they were introduced. I will state them; they will be in the recollection of the house, and I will endeavour to give an answer to them—in that answer, I will interweave some remarks, that may tend to illucidate the subject.

A good deal has already been said, concerning a bill of rights; I have stated, according to the best of my recollection, all that passed in convention, relating to that business. Since that time, I have spoken with a gentleman, who has not only his memory, but full notes, that he had taken in that body; and he assures me, that upon this subject, no direct motion was ever made at all; and certainly, before we heard this so violently supported out of doors, some pains ought to have been taken to have tried its fate within; but the truth is, a bill of rights would, as I have mentioned already, have been not only unnecessary but improper. In some governments it may come within the gentleman's idea, when he says it can do no harm; but even in these governments, you find bills of rights do not uniformly obtain; and do those states complain who have them not? Is it a maxim in forming governments, that not only all the powers which are given, but also that all those which are reserved, should be enumerated? I apprehend, that the powers given and reserved, form the whole rights of the people, as men and as citizens. I consider, that there are very few, who understand the *whole* of these rights. All the political writers, from Grotius and Puffendorf, down to Vattel, have treated on this subject; but in no one of those books, nor in the aggregate of them all, can you find a complete enumeration of rights, appertaining to the people as men and as citizens.

There are two kinds of government; that where general power is intended to be given to the legislature, and that, where the powers are particularly enumerated. In the last case, the implied result is, that nothing more is intended to be given, than what is so enumerated, unless it results from the nature of the government itself. On the other hand, when general legislative powers are given, then the people part with their authority, and on the gentleman's principle of government, retain nothing. But in a government like the proposed one, there can be no necessity for a bill of rights. For, on my principle, the people never part with their power. Enumerate all the rights of men!—I am sure, sir, that no gentleman in the late convention would have attempted such a thing. I believe the honorable speakers in opposition on this floor, were members of the assembly which appointed delegates to that convention; if it had been thought proper to have sent them into that body, how luminous would the *dark conclave* have been! So the gentleman has been pleased to denominate that body. Aristocrats as they were, they pretended not to define the rights of those who sent them there. We are asked repeatedly, what *harm* could the addition of a bill of rights do? If it can do no *good*, I think that a sufficient reason, to refuse having any thing to do with it. But to whom are we to report this bill of rights, if we should adopt it? Have we authority from those who sent us here to make one?

It is true we may propose, as well as any other private persons; but how shall we know the sentiments of the citizens of this state and of the other states? are we certain that any one of them will agree with our definitions and enumerations?

In the second place, we are told, that there is no check upon the government but the people; it is fortunate, sir, if their superintending authority is allowed as a check: But I apprehend that in the very construction of this government, there are numerous checks. Besides those expressly enumerated, the two branches of the legislature are mutual checks upon each other. But this subject will be more properly discussed, when we come to consider the form of government itself; and then I mean to shew the reason, why the right of habeas corpus was secured by a particular declaration in its favor.

In the third place we are told, that there is no security for the rights of conscience. I ask the honorable gentleman, what part of this system puts it in the power of congress to attack those rights? when there is no power to attack, it is idle to prepare the means of defence.

After having mentioned, in a cursory manner, the foregoing objections, we now arrive at the leading ones against the proposed system.

The very manner of introducing this constitution, by the recognition of the authority of the people, is said to change the principle of the present confederation, and to introduce a *consolidating* and absorbing government!

In this confederated republic, the sovereignty of the states, it is said, is not preserved. We are told, that there cannot be two sovereign powers, and that a subordinate sovereignty is no sovereignty.

It will be worth while, Mr. President, to consider this objection at large. When I had the honor of speaking formerly on this subject, I stated, in as concise a manner as possible, the leading ideas that occurred to me, to ascertain where the supreme and sovereign power resides. It has not been, nor, I presume, will it be denied, that somewhere there is, and of necessity must be, a supreme, absolute and uncontrolable authority. This, I believe, may justly be termed the sovereign power; for from that gentleman's (Mr. Findley) account of the matter, it cannot be sovereign, unless it is supreme; for, says he, a subordinate sovereignty is no sovereignty at all. I had the honor of observing, that if the question was asked, where the supreme power resided, different answers would be given by different writers. I mentioned, that Blackstone will tell you, that in Britain, it is lodged in the British parliament; and I believe there is no writer on this subject on the other side of the Atlantic, but supposes it to be vested in that body. I stated further, that if the question was asked, some politician, who had not considered the subject with sufficient accuracy, where the supreme power resided in our governments, he would answer, that it was vested in the state constitutions. This opinion approaches near the truth, but does not reach it; for the truth is, that the supreme, absolute and uncontrolable authority, *remains* with the people. I mentioned also, that the practical recognition of this truth was reserved for the honor of this country. I recollect no constitution founded on this principle. But we have witnessed the improvement, and enjoy the happiness, of seeing it carried into practice. The great and penetrating mind of Locke, seems to be the only one that pointed towards even the theory of this great truth.

When I made the observation, that some politicians would say the supreme power was lodged in our state constitutions, I did not suspect that the honorable gentleman from Westmoreland (Mr. Findley) was included in that description; but I find myself disappointed; for I imagined his opposition would arise from another consideration. His position is, that the supreme power resides in the states, as governments; and mine is, that it *resides* in the PEOPLE, as the fountain of government; that the people have not—that the people mean not—and that the people ought not, to part with it to any government whatsoever. In their hands it remains secure. They can delegate it in such proportions, to such bodies, on such terms, and under such limitations, as they think proper. I agree with the members in opposition, that there cannot be two sovereign powers on the same subject.

I consider the people of the United States, as forming one

great community; and I confider the people of the different states, as forming communities again on a lesser scale. From this great divifion of the people into diftinct communities, it will be found neceffary, that different proportions of legiflative powers fhould be given to the governments, according to the nature, number, and magnitude of their objects.

Unlefs the people are confidered in thefe two views, we fhall never be able to underftand the principle on which this fyftem was conftructed. I view the ftates as made *for* the People, as well as *by* them, and not the People as made for the ftates; the People, therefore, have a right, whilft enjoying the undeniable powers of fociety, to form either a general government, or ftate governments, in what manner they pleafe; or to accommodate them to one another; and by this means preferve them all; this, I fay, is the inherent and unalienable right of the people; and as an illuftration of it, I beg to read a few words from the declaration of independence, made by the reprefentatives of the United States, and recognized by the whole union.

" We hold thefe truths to be felf-evident, that all men are created equal; that they are endowed by their Creator with certain unalienable rights; that among thefe are life, liberty, and the purfuit of happinefs. That to fecure thefe rights, *governments* are inftituted among men, *deriving their juft powers from the confent of the governed*; that whenever any form of government becomes deftructive of thefe ends, it is the RIGHT of the People, to alter or to abolifh it, and inftitute new governments, laying its foundation on fuch principles, and organizing its powers in fuch forms, as to them fhall feem moft likely to effect their fafety and happinefs."

This is the broad bafis on which our independence was placed: on the fame certain and folid foundation this fyftem is erected.

State fovereignty, as it is called, is far from being able to fupport its weight. Nothing lefs than the authority of the people, could either fupport it, or give it efficacy. I cannot pafs over this fubject, without noticing the different conduct purfued by the late fœderal convention, and that obferved by the convention which framed the conftitution of Pennfylvania; on that occafion you find an attempt made to deprive the people of this right, fo lately and fo exprefsly afferted in the declaration of independence. We are told in the preamble to the declaration of rights, and frame of government, that *we* " do, by virtue of the authority vested in *us*, ordain, declare and establish, the following declaration of rights, and frame of government, to be the constitution of this commonwealth, and to remain in force therein UNALTERED, except in such articles as shall hereafter, on experience, be found to require improvement, and which shall, by the same authority of the people, fairly delegated *as this frame of government directs*"—An honorable gentleman, (Mr. Chambers) was well warranted in saying, that all that could be done, was done, to cut off the people from the right of amending; for if it be amended by any other mode than that which it directs, then any number more than one-third, may control any number less than two-thirds.

But I return to my general reasoning.—My position is, sir, that in this country the supreme, absolute, and uncontrolable power resides in the people at large; that they have vested certain proportions of this power in the state governments; but that the fee-simple continues, resides and remains, with the body of the people. Under the practical influence of this great truth, we are now sitting and deliberating, and under its operation, we can sit as calmly, and deliberate as coolly, in order to change a constitution, as a legislature can sit and deliberate under the power of a constitution, in order to alter or amend a law. It is true the exercise of this power will not probably be so frequent, nor resorted to on so many occasions in one case, as in the other: but the recognition of the principle cannot fail to establish it more firmly; because this recognition is made in the proposed constitution, an exception is taken to the whole of it: for we are told, it is a violation of the present confederation—a CONFEDERATION of SOVEREIGN STATES. I shall not enter into an investigation of the present confederation, but shall just remark, that its principle is not the principle of free governments. The PEOPLE of the United States are not as such represented in the present congress; and considered even as the component parts of the several states, they are not represented in proportion to their numbers and importance.

In this place I cannot help remarking, on the general inconsistency which appears between one part of the gentleman's objections and another. Upon the principle we have now mentioned, the honorable gentleman contended, that the powers ought to flow from the states; and that all the late convention had to do, was to give additional powers to congress. What is the present form of congress? A single body, with some legislative, but little executive, and no effective judicial power. What are these additional powers that are to be given? In some cases legislative are wanting, in others judicial, and in others executive; these, it is said, ought to be allotted to the general government; but the impropriety of delegating such extensive trust to one body of men is evident; yet in the same day, and perhaps in the same hour, we are told, by honorable gentlemen, that these three branches of government are not kept sufficiently distinct in this constitution; we are told also that the senate, possessing some executive power, as well as legislative, is such a monster that it will swallow up and absorb every other body in the general government, after having destroyed those of the particular states.

Is this reasoning with consistency? Is the senate under the proposed constitution so tremendous a body, when checked in their legislative capacity by the house of representatives, and in their executive authority, by the president of the United States? Can this body be so tremendous as the present congress, a single body of men possessed of legislative, executive and judicial powers? to what purpose was Montesquieu read to shew that this was a complete tyranny? the application would have been more properly made by the advocates of the proposed constitution, against the patrons of the present confederation.

It is mentioned that this fœderal government will annihilate and absorb all the state governments. I wish to save as much as possible the time of the house, I shall not, therefore, recapitulate what I had the honor of saying last week on this subject; I hope it was then shewn, that instead of being abolished (as insinuated) from the very nature of things, and from the organization of the system itself, the state governments must exist, or the general government must fall amidst their ruins; indeed so far as to the forms, it is admitted they may remain; but the gentlemen seem to think their power will be gone.

I shall have occasion to take notice of this power hereafter, and, I believe, if it was necessary, it could be shewn that the state governments, as states, will enjoy as much power, and more dignity, happiness and security, than they have hitherto done. I admit, sir, that some of the powers will be taken from them, by the system before you; but it is, I believe, allowed on all hands, at least it is not among us a disputed point, that the late convention was appointed with a particular view to give more power to the government of the union: it is also acknowled, that the intention was to obtain the advantage of an efficient government over the United States; now, if power is to be given to that government, I apprehend it must be taken from some place: If the state governments are to retain all the powers they held before, then, of consequence, every new power that is given to congress must be taken from the people at large. Is this the gentleman's intention? I believe a strict examination of this subject will justify me in asserting, that the states, as governments, have assumed too much power to themselves, while they left little to the people. Let not this be called cajoling the people—the elegant expression used by the honorable gentleman from Westmoreland (Mr. Findley) it is hard to avoid censure on one side or the other. At some time it has been said, that I have not been at the pains to conceal my contempt of the people; but when it suits a purpose better, it is asserted that I cajole them. I do neither one nor the other. The voice of approbation, sir, when I think that approbation well earned, I confess is grateful to my ears; but I would disdain it, if it is to be purchased by a sacrifice of my duty, or the dictates of my conscience. No, sir, I go practically into this system, I have gone into it practically when the doors were shut; when it could not be alleged that I cajoled the people, and I now endeavour to shew that the true and only safe principle for a free people, is a practical recognition of their original and supreme authority.

I say, sir, that it was the design of this system, to take some power from the state government, and to place it in the general government. It was also the design, that the people should be admitted to the exercise of some powers, which they did not exercise under the present confederation. It was thought proper, that the citizens, as well as the states should be represented; how far the representation in the senate is a representation of states, we shall see by and by, when we come to consider that branch of the fœderal government.

This system, it is said, "unhinges and eradicates the state governments, and was systematically intended so to do;" to establish the *intention*, an argument is drawn from Art. 1st sect. 4th on the subject of elections. I have already had occasion to remark upon this, and shall therefore pass on to the next objection.

That the last clause of the 8th sect. of the 1st article, gives the power of self-preservation to the general government, *independent* of the states. For in case of their *abolition*, it will be alleged in behalf of the general government, that self-preservation is the first law, and necessary to the exercise of *all other* powers.

Now let us see what this objection amounts to. Who are to have this self-preserving power? the congress. Who are congress? it is a body that will consist of a senate and a house of representatives. Who compose this senate? those who are *elected* by the *legislatures* of the different states. Who are the electors of the house of representatives? Those who are *qualified* to *vote* for the most numerous branch of the *legislature* in the separate states. Suppose the state legislatures annihilated, where is the criterion to ascertain the qualification of electors? and unless this be ascertained, they cannot be admitted to vote; if a state legislature is not elected, there can be no senate, because the senators are to be chosen by the *legislatures only*.

This is a plain and simple deduction from the constitution, and yet the objection is stated as conclusive upon an argument expressly drawn from the last clause of this section.

It is repeated, with confidence, " that this is not a *fæderal* government, but a complete one, with legislative, executive and judicial powers : It is a *consolidating* government." I have already mentioned the misuse of the term ; I wish the gentleman would indulge us with his definition of the word. If, when he says it is a consolidation, he means so far as relates to the general objects of the union—so far it was intended to be a consolidation, and on such a consolidation, perhaps our very existence, as a nation, depends. If, on the other hand (as something which has been said seems to indicate) he (Mr. Findley) means that it will absorb the governments of the individual states, so far is this position from being admitted, that it is unanswerably controverted. The existence of the state government, is one of the most prominent features of this system. With regard to those pur-

which are allowed to be for the general welfare of the union, I think it no objection to this plan, that we are told it is a complete government. I think it no objection, that it is alleged the government will possess legislative, executive and judicial powers. Should it have only legislative authority! we have had examples enough of such a government, to deter us from continuing it. Shall congress any longer continue to make requisitions from the several states, to be treated sometimes with silent and sometimes with declared contempt? For what purpose give the power to make laws, unless they are to be executed? and if they are to be executed, the executive and judicial powers will necessarily be engaged in the business.

Do we wish a return of those insurrections and tumults to which a sister state was lately exposed? or a government of such insufficiency as the present is found to be? Let me, sir, mention one circumstance in the recollection of every honorable gentleman who hears me. To the determination of congress are submitted all disputes between states, concerning boundary, jurisdiction, or right of soil. In consequence of this power, after much altercation, expence of time, and considerable expence of money, this state was successful enough to obtain a decree in her favour, in a difference then subsisting between her and Connecticut; but what was the consequence? the congress had no power to carry the decree into execution. Hence the distraction and animosity, which have ever since prevailed, and still continue in that part of the country. Ought the government then to remain any longer incomplete? I hope not; no person can be so insensible to the lessons of experience as to desire it.

It is brought as an objection "that there will be a rivalship between the state governments and the general government; on each side endeavours will be made to increase power."

Let us examine a little into this subject. The gentlemen tell you, sir, that they expect the states will not possess any power. But I think there is reason to draw a different conclusion. Under this system their respectability and power will increase with that of the general government. I believe their happiness and security will increase in a still greater proportion; let us attend a moment to the situation of this country, it is a maxim of every government, and it ought to be a maxim with us, that the increase of numbers increa-
he dignity, the security, and the respectability of all go-

vernments; it is the firſt command given by the Deity to man, increaſe and multiply; this applies with peculiar force to this country, the ſmaller part of whoſe terrotory is yet inhabited. We are repreſentatives, ſir, not merely of the preſent age, but of future times; not merely of the territory along the ſea coaſt, but of regions immenſely extended weſtward. We ſhould fill, as faſt as poſſible, this extenſive country, with men who ſhall live happy, free and ſecure. To accompliſh this great end ought to be the leading view of all our patriots and ſtateſmen. But how is it to be accompliſhed, but by eſtabliſhing peace and harmony among ourſelves, and dignity and reſpectability among foreign nations. By theſe means, we may draw numbers from the other ſide of the atlantic, in addition to the natural ſources of population. Can either of theſe objects be attained without a protecting head?—When we examine hiſtory, we ſhall find an important fact, and almoſt the only fact, which will apply to all confederacies.

They have all fallen to pieces, and have not abſorbed the ſubordinate government.

In order to keep republics together they muſt have a ſtrong binding force, which muſt be either external or internal. The ſituation of this country ſhews, that no foreign force can preſs us together, the bonds of our union ought therefore to be indiſſolubly ſtrong.

The powers of the ſtates, I apprehend, will increaſe with the population, and the happineſs of their inhabitants. Unleſs we can eſtabliſh a character abroad, we ſhall be unhappy from foreign reſtraints, or internal violence. Theſe reaſons, I think, prove ſufficiently the neceſſity of having a federal head. Under it the advantages enjoyed by the whole union would be participated by every ſtate. I wiſh honorable gentlemen would think not only of themſelves, not only of the preſent age, but of others, and of future times.

It has been ſaid, "that the ſtate governments will not be able to make head againſt the general government," but it might be ſaid with more propriety, that the general government will not be able to maintain the powers given it againſt the encroachments and combined attacks of the ſtates governments. They poſſeſs ſome particular advantages, from which the general government is reſtrained. By this ſyſtem, there is a proviſion made in the conſtitution, that, no ſenator or repreſentative, ſhall be appointed to any civil office under the authority of the United States, which ſhall have been created, or the emoluments whereof shall have been increased, during the time for which he was elected; and no person holding any office under the United States can be a member of either house; but there is no similar security against state influence, as a representative may enjoy places, and even sinecures under the state governments. On which side is the door most open to corruption? if a person in the legislature is to be influenced by an office, the general government can give him none unless he vacate his seat. When the influence of office comes from the state government, he can retain his seat and salary too. But, it is added, under this head "that state governments will lose the attachment "of the people, by losing the power of conferring advan- "tages, and that the people will not be at the expence of "keeping them up." Perhaps the state governments have already become so expensive as to alarm the gentlemen on that head. I am told that the civil list of this state amounted to £. 40,000, in one year. Under the proposed government, I think it would be possible to obtain in Pennsylvania every advantage we now possess, with a civil list that shall not exceed one-third of that sum.

How differently the same thing is talked of, if it be a favorite or otherwise! when advantages to an officer are to be derived from the general government, we hear them mentioned by the name of *bribery*, but when we are told of the states governments losing the power of conferring advantages, by the disposal of offices, it is said they will loose the *attachment* of the people: What is in one instance corruption and bribery, is in another the power of conferring advantages.

We are informed "that the state elections will be ill attended, and that the state governments will become mere boards of electors." Those who have a due regard for their country, will discharge their duty, and attend; but those who are brought only from interest or persuasion had better stay away; the public will not suffer any disadvantage from their absence. But the honest citizens, who know the value of the privilege, will undoubtedly attend, to secure the man of his choice. The power and business of the state legislatures relates to the great objects of life liberty and property, the same are also objects of the general government.

Certainly the citizens of America will be as tenacious in the one instance as in the other. They will be interested, and I hope will exert themselves, to secure their rights not only from being injured by the ſtate governments, but alſo from being injured by the general government.

"The power over election, and of judging of elections, gives abſolute ſovereignty," this power is given to every ſtate legiſlature, yet I ſee no neceſſity, that the power of abſolute ſovereignty ſhould accompany it. My general poſition is, that the abſolute ſovereignty never goes from the people.

We are told, "that it will be in the power of the ſenate to prevent any addition of repreſentatives to the lower houſe."

I believe their power will be pretty well balanced, and though the ſenate ſhould have a deſire to do this, yet the attempt will anſwer no purpoſe; for the houſe of repreſentatives will not let them have a farthing of public money, till they agree to it. And the latter influence will be as ſtrong as the other.

"Annual aſſemblies are neceſſary" it is ſaid—and I anſwer in many inſtances they are very proper.—In Rhode-Iſland and Connecticut they are elected for ſix months. In larger ſtates, that period would be found very inconvenient, but in a government as large as that of the United States, I preſume that annual elections would be more diſproportionate, than elections for ſix months would be in ſome of our largeſt ſtates.

"The Britiſh parliament took to themſelves the prolongation of their ſitting to ſeven years. But even in the Britiſh parliament the appropriations are annual."

But, ſir, how is the argument to apply here?—how are the congreſs to aſſume ſuch a power? they cannot aſſume it under the conſtitution, for that expreſſly provides "the members of the houſe of repreſentatives ſhall be choſen every two years, by the people of the ſeveral ſtates, and the ſenators for ſix years." So if they take it at all, they muſt take it by uſurpation and force.

"Appropriations may be made for two years,—though in the Britiſh parliament they are made but for one,"—for ſome purpoſes, ſuch appropriations may be made annually, but for every purpoſe they are not; even for a ſtanding army, they may be made for ſeven, ten, or fourteen years—the civil liſt is eſtabliſhed, during the life of a prince.—Another objection is "that the members of the ſenate may enrich themſelves—they may hold their office as long as they live, and there is no power to prevent them; the ſenate will ſwallow up every thing"—I am not a blind admirer of this fyſtem. Some of the powers of the ſenators are not with me the favorite parts of it, but as they ſtand connected with other parts, there is ſtill ſecurity againſt the efforts of that body: it was with great difficulty that ſecurity was obtained, and I may riſque the conjecture, that if it is not now accepted, it never will be obtained again from the ſame ſtates. Though the ſenate was not a favorite of mine, as to ſome of its powers, yet it was a favorite with a majority in the union, and we muſt ſubmit to that majority, or we muſt break up the union. It is but fair to repeat thoſe reaſons, that weighed with the convention; perhaps, I ſhall not be able to do them juſtice, but yet I will attempt to ſhew, why additional powers were given to the ſenate, rather than to the houſe of repreſentatives. Theſe additional powers, I believe, are, that of trying impeachments, that of concurring with the preſident in making treaties, and that of concurring in the appointment of officers. Theſe are the powers that are ſtated as improper. It is fortunate, that in the exerciſe of every one of them, the ſenate ſtands controlled; if it is that monſter which it ſaid to be, it can only ſhew its teath; it is unable to bite or devour: With regard to impeachments, the ſenate can try none but ſuch as will be brought before them by the houſe of repreſentatives.

The ſenate can make no treaties; they can approve of none unleſs the preſident of the United States lay it before them. With regard to the appointment of officers, the preſident muſt nominate before they can vote: So that if the powers of either branch are perverted, it muſt be with the approbation of ſome one of the other branches of government: thus checked on each ſide, they can do noo ne act of themſelves.

"The powers of congreſs extend to taxation---to direct taxation---to internal taxation---to poll taxes---to exciſes---to other ſtate and internal purpoſes." Thoſe who poſſeſs the power to tax, poſſeſs all other ſovereign power. That their powers are thus extenſive is admitted; and would any thing ſhort of this have been ſufficient? is it the wiſh of theſe gentlemen? if it is let us hear their ſentiments---that the general government ſhould ſubſiſt on the bounty of the ſtates. Shall it have the power to contract, and no power to fulfil the contract? Shall it have the power to borrow money, and no power to pay the principal or interest? Must we go on, in the tract that we have hitherto pursued? and must we again compel those in Europe, who lent us money in our distress, to advance the money to pay themselves interest on the certificates of the debts due to them?

This was actually the case in Holland, the last year.—Like those who have shot one arrow, and cannot regain it, they have been obliged to shoot another in the same direction, in order to recover the first. It was absolutely necessary, sir, that this government should possess these rights, and why should it not as well as the state governments? Will this government be fonder of the exercise of this authority, than those of the states are? Will the states, who are equally represented in one branch of the legislature, be more opposed to the payment of what shall be required by the future, than what has been required by the present congress? Will the people, who must indisputably pay the whole, have more objections to the payment of this tax, because it is laid by persons of their own immediate appointment, even if those taxes were to continue as oppressive as they now are?—but under the general power of this system, that cannot be the case in Pennsylvania. Throughout the union, direct taxation will be lessened, at least in proportion to the encrease of the other objects of revenue.—In this constitution, a power is given to congress to collect imposts, which is not given by the present articles of confederation. A very considerable part of the revenue of the United States will arise from that source; it is the easiest, most just, and most productive mode of raising revenue; and it is a safe one, because it is voluntary. No man is obliged to consume more than he pleases, and each buys in proportion only to his consumption. The price of the commodity is blended with the tax, and the person is often not sensible of the payment. But would it have been proper to have rested the matter there? Suppose this fund should not prove sufficient, ought the public debts to remain unpaid? Or the exigencies of government be left unprovided for? Should our tranquillity be exposed to the assaults of foreign enemies, or violence among ourselves, because the objects of commerce may not furnish a sufficient revenue to secure them all? Certainly congress should possess the power of raising revenue from their constituents, for the purpose mentioned in the eighth section of the first article, that is " to pay the debts and provide for the common defence and general welfare of the United States." It has been common, with the gentlemen on this subject, to present us with frightful pictures. We are told of the hosts of tax-gatherers that will swarm through the land; and whenever taxes are mentioned, military force seems to be an attending idea. I think I may venture to predict, that the taxes of the general government (if any shall be laid) will be more equitable, and much less expensive, than those imposed by the state government.

I shall not go into an investigation of this subject; but it must be confessed, that scarcely any mode of laying and collecting taxes can be more burdensome than the present.

Another objection is, "that congress may borrow money, keep up standing armies, and command the militia:" The present congress possesses the power of borrowing money and of keeping up standing armies. Whether it will be proper at all times to keep up a body of troops, will be a question to be determined by congress; but I hope the necessity will not subsist at all times; but if it should subsist, where is the gentleman that will say that they ought not to possess the necessary power of keeping them up?

It is urged, as a general objection to this system, that "the powers of congress are unlimitted and undefined, and that they will be the judges, in all cases, of what is necessary and proper for them to do." To bring this subject to your view, I need do no more than point to the words in the constitution, beginning at the 8th sect. art. 1st. "The congress (it says) shall have power, &c." I need not read over the words, but I leave it to every gentleman to say whether the powers are not as accurately and minutely defined, as can be well done on the same subject, in the same language. The old constitution is as strongly marked on this subject; and even the concluding clause, with which so much fault has been found, gives no more, or other powers; nor does it in any degree go beyond the particular enumeration; for when it is said, that congress shall have power to make all laws which shall be necessary and proper, those words are limitted, and defined by the following, "for carrying into execution the foregoing powers." It is saying no more than that the powers we have already particularly given, shall be effectually carried into execution.

I shall not detain the house, at this time, with any further observations on the liberty of the press, until it is shewn that congress have any power whatsoever to interfere with it, by licensing it, or declaring what shall be a libel.

I proceed to another objection, which was not so fully stated as I believe it will be hereafter; I mean the objection against the judicial department. The gentleman from Westmoreland only mentioned it to illustrate his objection to the legislative department. He said " that the judicial powers were co-extensive with the legislative powers, and extend even to capital cases." I believe they ought to be co-extensive, otherwise laws would be framed, that could not be executed. Certainly, therefore, the executive and judicial departments ought to have power commensurate to the extent of the laws; for, as I have already asked, are we to give power to *make* laws, and no power to *carry them into effect?*

I am happy to mention the punishment annexed to one crime. You will find the current running strong in favour of humanity. For this is the first instance in which it has not been left to the legislature, to extend the crime and punishment of treason so far as they thought proper. This punishment, and the description of this crime, are the great sources of danger and persecution, on the part of government against the citizen. Crimes against the state! and against the officers of the state! History informs us, that more wrong may be done on this subject than on any other whatsoever. But under this constitution, there can be no treason against the United States, except such as is defined in this constitution. The manner of trial is clearly pointed out; the positive testimony of two witnesses to the same overt act, or a confession in open court, is required to convict any person of treason. And after all, the consequences of the crime shall extend no further than the life of the criminal; for no attainder of treason shall work corruption of blood, or forfeiture, except during the life of the person attainted.

I come now to consider the last set of objections that are offered against this constitution. It is urged, that this is not such a system as was within the powers of the convention; they assumed the *power of proposing*. I believe they might have made proposals without going beyond their powers. I never heard before, that to make a proposal was an exercise of power. But if it is an exercise of power, they certainly did assume it; yet they did not act as that body who framed the present constitution of Pennsylvania acted; they did not by an ordinance, attempt to rivet the constitution or

the people, before they could vote for members of assembly under it. Yet such was the effect of the ordinance that attended the constitution of this commonwealth. I think the late convention have done nothing beyond their powers. The fact is, they have exercised no power at all. And in point of validity, this constitution, proposed by them for the government of the United States, claims no more than a production of the same nature would claim, flowing from a private pen. It is laid before the citizens of the United States, unfettered by restraint; it is laid before them, to be judged by the natural, civil and political rights of men. By their FIAT, it will become of value and authority; without it, it will never receive the character of authenticity and power. The business, we are told, which was entrusted to the late convention, was merely to amend the present articles of confederation. This observation has been frequently made, and has often brought to my mind, a story that is related of Mr. Pope, who it is well known, was not a little deformed. It was customary with him, to use this phrase, " God mend me," when any little accident happened. One evening a link boy was lighting him along, and coming to a gutter, the boy jumped nimbly over it—Mr. Pope called to him to turn, adding, " God mend me:" The arch rogue turned to light him—looked at him, and repeated ", God mend you! he would sooner make half-a-dozen new ones." This would apply to the present confederation; for it would be easier to make another than to mend this. The gentlemen urge, that this is such a government as was not expected by the people, the legislatures, nor by the honorable gentlemen who mentioned it. Perhaps it was not such as was expected, *but it may be* BETTER; and is that a reason why it should not be adopted? it is not worse, I trust, than the former. So that the argument of its being a system not expected, is an argument more strong in its favour than against it. The letter which accompanies this constitution, must strike every person with the utmost force. " The friends of
" our country have long seen and desired the power of war,
" peace, and treaties, that of levying money and regulating
" commerce, and the corresponding executive and judicial
" authorities, should be fully and effectually vested in the
" general government of the union; but the impropriety of
" delegating such extensive trust to one body of men, is evi-
" dent. *Hence results the necessity of a different organiza-*

" *tion.*" I therefore do not think that it can be urged as an objection againſt this ſyſtem, that it was not expected by the people. We are told, to add greater force to theſe objections, that they are not on local, but on general principles, and that they are uniform throughout the United States. I confeſs I am not altogether of that opinion; I think ſome of the objections are inconſiſtent with others, ariſing from a different quarter, and I think ſome are inconſiſtent, even with thoſe derived from the ſame ſource. But, on this occaſion, let us take the fact for granted, that they are all on general principles, and uniform throughout the United States.— Then we can judge of their full amount; and what are they, BUT TRIFLES LIGHT AS AIR? We ſee the whole force of them; for according to the ſentiments of oppoſition, they can no where be ſtronger, or more fully ſtated than here. The concluſion, from all theſe objections, is reduced to a point, and the plan is declared to be inimical to our liberties. I have ſaid nothing, and mean to ſay nothing, concerning the diſpoſitions or characters of thoſe that framed the work now before you. I agree that it ought to be judged by its own intrinſic qualities. If it has not merit, weight of character ought not to carry it into effect. On the other hand, if it has merit, and is calculated to ſecure the bleſſings of liberty, and to promote the general welfare, then ſuch objections as have hitherto been made ought not to influence us to reject it.

I am now led to conſider thoſe qualities that this ſyſtem of government poſſeſſes, which will entitle it to the attention of the United States. But as I have ſomewhat fatigued myſelf, as well as the patience of the honorable members of this houſe, I ſhall defer what I have to add on this ſubject until the afternoon.

EODEM DIE, P. M.

MR. WILSON.

Before I proceed to conſider thoſe qualities in the conſtitution before us, which I think will enſure it our approbation, permit me to make ſome remarks, and they ſhall be very conciſe, upon the objections that were offered this forenoon, by the member from Fayette (Mr. Smilie.) I do it, at this time, becauſe I think it will be better to give a ſatisfactory anſwer to the whole of the objections, before I proceed to the other part of my subject. I find that the doctrine of a single legislature is not to be contended for in this constitution. I shall therefore say nothing on that point. I shall consider that part of the system, when we come to view its excellencies. Neither shall I take particular notice of his observation on the qualified negative of the president; for he finds no fault with it; he mentions, however, that he thinks it a vain and useless power, because it can never be executed. The reason he assigns for this is, that the king of Great-Britain, who has an absolute negative over the laws proposed by parliament, has never exercised it, at least, not for many years. It is true, and the reason why he did not exercise it, was, that during all that time, the king possessed a negative before the bill had passed through the two houses ; a much stronger power than a negative after debate. I believe, since the revolution, at the time of William the IIId. it was never known, that a bill disagreeable to the crown, passed both houses. At one time in the reign of Queen Anne, when there appeared some danger of this being effected, it is well known that she created twelve peers, and by that means effectually defeated it.—Again; there was some risk of late years in the present reign, with regard to Mr. Fox's East-India bill, as it is usually called, that passed through the house of commons, but the king had interest enough in the house of peers, to have it thrown out; thus it never came up for the royal assent. But that is no reason why this negative should not be exercised here, and exercised with great advantage. Similar powers are known in more than one of the states. The governors of Massachusetts and New-York have a power similar to this; and it has been exercised frequently to good effect.

I believe the governor of New-York, under this power, has been known to send back five or six bills in a week; and I well recollect that at the time the funding system was adopted by our legislature, the people in that state considered the negative of the governor as a great security, that their legislature would not be able to incumber them by a similar measure. Since that time an alteration has been supposed in the governor's conduct, but there has been no alteration in his power.

The honorable gentleman from Westmoreland (Mr. Findley) by his highly refined critical abilities, discovers an inconfiftency in this part of the conftitution, and that which declares in fection firft: "All legiflative powers, herein "granted, fhall be vefted in a congrefs of the United States, "which fhall confift of a fenate and a houfe of reprefenta- "tives," and yet here, fays he, is a power of legiflation given to the prefident of the United States, becaufe every bill, before it becomes a law, fhall be prefented to him: Thus he is faid to poffefs legiflative powers. Sir, the convention obferved on this occafion ftrict propriety of language; "if he approve the bill when it is fent, he fhall fign it, but if not he fhall return it;" but no bill paffes in confequence of having his affent—therefore he poffeffes no legiflative authority.

The effect of his power, upon this fubject, is merely this, if he difapproves a bill, two-thirds of the legiflature become neceffary, to pafs it into a law, inftead of a bare majority. And when two-thirds are in favor of the bill, it becomes a law, not by his, but by authority of the two houfes of the legiflature. We are told, in the next place, by the honorable gentleman from Fayette (Mr. Smilie) that in the different orders of mankind, there is that of a natural ariftocracy. On fome occafions, there is a kind of magical expreffion, ufed to conjure up ideas, that may create uneafinefs and apprehenfion. I hope the meaning of the words is underftood by the gentleman who ufed them.—I have afked repeatedly of gentlemen to explain, but have not been able to obtain the explanation of what they meant by a confolidated government.—They keep round and round about the thing, but never define. I afk now what is meant by a natural ariftocracy? I am not at a lofs for the etymological definition of the term, for, when we trace it to the language from which it is derived, an ariftocracy means nothing more or lefs than a government of the beft men in the community, or thofe who are recommended by the words of the conftitution of Pennfylvania, where it is directed, that the reprefentatives fhould confift of thofe moft noted for wifdom and virtue. Is there any danger in fuch reprefentation? I fhall never find fault, that fuch characters are employed. Happy for us, when fuch characters can be obtained.—If this is meant by a natural ariftocracy, and I know no other, can it be objectionable, that men fhould be employed that are moft noted for their virtue and talents?—And are attempts made to mark out thefe as the moft improper perfons for the public confidence?

I had the honor of giving a definition, and I believe it was a juft one, of what is called an ariftocratic government. It is a government where the fupreme power is not retained by the people, but refides in a felect body of men, who either fill up the vacancies that happen, by their own choice and election, or fucceed on the principle of defcent, or by virtue of territorial poffeffions, or fome other qualifications that are not the refult of perfonal properties. When I fpeak of perfonal properties, I mean the qualities of the head and the difpofition of the heart.

We are told that the reprefentatives will not be known to the people, nor the people to the reprefentatives, becaufe they will be taken from large diftricts where they cannot be particularly acquainted. There has been fome experience in feveral of the ftates, upon this fubject, and I believe the experience of all who have had experience, demonftrates that the larger the diftrict of election, the better the reprefentation. It is only in remote corners of a government, that little demagogues arife. Nothing but real weight of character, can give a man real influence over a large diftrict. This is remarkably fhewn in the commonwealth of Maffachufetts. The members of the houfe of reprefentatives, are chofen in very fmall diftricts, and fuch has been the influence of party cabal and little intrigue in them, that a great majority feem inclined to fhew very little difapprobation of the conduct of the infurgents in that ftate.

The governor is chofen by the people at large, and that ftate is much larger than any diftrict need be under the propofed conftitution. In their choice of their governor, they have had warm difputes; but however warm the difputes, their choice only vibrated between the moft eminent characters. Four of their candidates are well known; Mr. Hancock, Mr. Bowdoin, general Lincoln, and Mr. Gorham, the late prefident of congrefs.

I apprehend it is of more confequence to be able to know the true intereft of the people, than their faces, and of more confequence ftill, to have virtue enough to purfue the means of carrying that knowledge ufefully into effect. And furely when it has been thought hitherto, that a reprefentation in congrefs of from five to two members, was fufficient to reprefent the intereft of this ftate, is it not more than fufficient to have ten members in that body? and thofe in greater comparative proportion than heretofore? The ci-
ns of Pennfylvania will be reprefented by eight, and the

state by two. This, certainly, though not gaining enough, is gaining a good deal; the members will be more diftributed through the ftate, being the immediate choice of the people, who hitherto have not been reprefented in that body. It is said that the houfe of reprefentatives will be fubject to corruption, and the fenate poffefs the means of corrupting, by the fhare they have in the appointment to office. This was not fpoken in the foft language of attachment to government. It is perhaps impoffible, with all the caution of legiflators and ftatefmen, to exclude corruption and undue influence entirely from government. All that can be done, upon this fubject, is done in the conftitution before you. Yet it behoves us to call out, and add, every guard and preventative in our power. I think, fir, fomething very important, on this fubject, is done in the prefent fyftem. For it has been provided, effectually, that the man that has been bribed by an office, fhall have it no longer in his power to earn his wages. The moment he is engaged to ferve the fenate, in confequence of their gift, he no longer has it in his power to fit in the houfe of reprefentatives. For "no reprefentative fhall, during the term for which he was elected, be appointed to any civil office, under the authority of the United States, which fhall have been created, or the emoluments whereof fhall have been encreafed during fuch time:" And the following annihilates corruption of that kind. "And no perfon holding any office under the United States, fhall be a member of either houfe, during his continuance in office." So that the mere acceptance of an office as a bribe, effectually deftroys the end for which it was offered. Was this attended to when it was mentioned, that the members of the one houfe could be bribed by the other? "But the members of the fenate may enrich themfelves," was an obfervation, made as an objection to this fyftem. As the mode of doing this has not been pointed out, I apprehend the objection is not much relied upon. The fenate are incapable of receiving any money, except what is paid them out of the public treafury. They cannot vote to themfelves a fingle penny, unlefs the propofition originates from the other houfe. This objection therefore is vifionary, like the following one, "that pictured groupe, that numerous hoft, and prodigious fwarm of officers, which are to be appointed under the general government." The gentlemen

L

tell you that there muft be judges of the fupreme, and judges of the inferior courts, with all their appendages:—there will be tax-gatherers fwarming throughout the land. Oh! fay they, if we could enumerate the offices, and the numerous officers that muft be employed every day, in collecting and receiving, and comptrolling the monies of the United States, the number would be almoft beyond imagination. I have been told, but I do not vouch for the fact, that there are in one fhape or another, more than a thoufand perfons in this very ftate, who get their living in affeffing and collecting our revenues from the other citizens. Sir, when this bufinefs of revenue is conducted on a general plan, we may be able to do the bufinefs of the thirteen ftates, with an equal, nay, with a lefs number—inftead of thirteen comptroller generals, one comptroller will be fufficient; I apprehend, that the number of officers, under this fyftem, will be greatly reduced from the number now employed. For as congrefs can now do nothing effectually, the ftates are obliged to do every thing. And in this very point, I apprehend, that we fhall be great gainers.

Sir, I confefs I wifh the powers of the fenate were not as they are. I think it would have been better if thofe powers had been diftributed in other parts of the fyftem. I mentioned fome circumftances in the forenoon, that I had obferved on this fubject. I may mention now, we may think ourfelves very well off, fir, that things are as well as they are, and that that body is given fo much reftricted. But furely objections of this kind come with a bad grace from the advocates, or thofe who prefer the prefent confederation, and who wifh only to encreafe the powers of the prefent congrefs. A fingle body not conftituted with checks, like the propofed one, who poffefs not only the power of making treaties, but executive powers, would be a perfect defpotifm; but, further, thefe powers are, in the prefent confederation, poffeffed without control.

As I mentioned before, fo I will beg leave to repeat, that this fenate can do nothing without the concurrence of fome other branch of the government. With regard to their concern in the appointment to offices, the prefident muft nominate before they can be chofen; the prefident muft acquiefce in that appointment. With regard to their power in forming treaties, they can make none, they are only auxiliaries to the prefident. They muft try all impeachments but they have no power to try any until prefented by th houfe of reprefentatives; and when I confider this fubjec though I wifh the regulations better, I think no danger to th liberties of this country can arife even from that part of th fyftem. But thefe objections, I fay, come with a bad grac from thofe who prefer the prefent confederation, who thir it only neceffary to add more powers to a body organized i that form. I confefs, likewife, that by combining thofe pov ers, of trying impeachments, and making treaties, in tl fame body, it will not be fo eafy as I think it ought to b to call the fenators to an account for any improper condu in that bufinefs.

Thofe who propofed this fyftem, were not inattentive do all they could. I admit the force of the obfervation, ma by the gentleman from Fayette (Mr. Smilie) that when tw thirds of the fenate concur in forming a bad treaty, it w be hard to procure a vote of two-thirds againft them, they fhould be impeached. I think fuch a thing is not be expected; and fo far they are without that *immediate* d gree of refponfibility, which I think requifite, to make tl part of the work perfect. But this will not be *always* t cafe. When a member of fenate fhall behave criminally, t criminality will not expire with his office. The fenat may be called to account after they fhall have been chang and the body to which they belonged fhall have been alter There is a rotation; and every fecond year one third of t whole number go out. Every fourth year two thirds them are changed. In fix years the whole body is fuppl by a new one. Confidering it in this view, refponfibility not entirely loft. There is another view in which it ou to be confidered, which will fhew that we have a grea degree of fecurity. Though they may not be convicted on i peachment before the fenate, they may be tried by their co try: and if their criminality is eftablifhed, the law will nifh. A grand jury may prefent, a petty Jury may convict, the judges will pronounce the punifhment. This is all t can be done under the prefent confederation, for undei there is no power of impeachment; even here then we g fomething. Thofe parts that are exceptionable in this c ftitution, are improvements on that concerning which much pains are taken to perfuade us, that it is preferabl the other.

The laſt obſervation reſpects the judges. It is ſaid that if they dare' to decide againſt the law, one houſe will impeach them, and the other will convict them. I hope gentlemen will ſhew how this can happen, for bare ſuppoſition ought not to be admitted as proof. The judges are to be impeached, becauſe they decide an act null and void, that was made in defiance of the conſtitution! What houſe of repreſentatives would dare to impeach, or ſenate to commit judges for the performance of their duty? Theſe obſervations are of a ſimilar kind to thoſe with regard to the liberty of the preſs.

I will now proceed to take ſome notice of thoſe qualities in this conſtitution, that I think entitle it to our reſpect and favour. I have not yet done, ſir, with the great principle on which it ſtands; I mean the practical recognition of this doctrine, that in the United States the people retain the ſupreme power.

In giving a definition of the ſimple kinds of government known throughout the world, I had occaſion to deſcribe what I meant by a democracy; and I think I termed it, that government in which the people retain the ſupreme power, and exerciſe it either collectively or by repreſentation—this conſtitution declares this principle in its terms and in its conſequences, which is evident from the manner in which it is announced. "WE, THE PEOPLE OF THE UNITED STATES. After all the examination, which I am able to give the ſubject, I view this as the only ſufficient and the moſt honorable baſis, both for the people and government, on which our conſtitution can poſſibly reſt. What are all the contrivances of ſtates, of kingdoms and empires?—What are they all intended for? They are all intended for man, and our natural character and natural rights are certainly to take place, in preference to all artificial refinements that human wiſdom can deviſe.

I am aſtoniſhed to hear the ill-founded doctrine, that ſtates alone ought to be repreſented in the federal government; theſe muſt poſſeſs ſovereign authority forſooth, and the people be forgot—No—Let us *reaſcend* to firſt principles— That expreſſion is not ſtrong enough to do my ideas juſtice.

Let us RETAIN firſt principles. The people of the United States are now in the poſſeſſion and exerciſe of their original rights, and while this doctrine is known, and operates, we ſhall have a cure for every diſeaſe.

I shall mention another good quality, belonging to this system.----In it the legislative, executive and judicial powers, are kept nearly independent and distinct. I express myself in this guarded manner, because I am aware of some powers that are blended in the senate. They are but few; and they are not dangerous. It is an exception, yet that exception consists of but few instances, and none of them dangerous.—I believe in no constitution for any country on earth is this great principle so strictly adhered to, or marked with so much precision and accuracy, as in this. It is much more accurate, than that which the honorable gentleman so highly extols, I mean the constitution of England.—There, sir, one branch of the legislature can appoint the members of another. The king has the power of introducing members into the house of Lords. I have already mentioned that in order to obtain a vote, twelve peers were poured into that house at one time; the operation is the same, as might be under this constitution, if the president had a right to appoint the members of the senate. This power of the king's extends into the other branch, where, though he cannot immediately introduce a member, yet he can do it remotely by virtue of his prerogative, as he may create boroughs with power to send members to the house of commons. The house of lords form a much stronger exception to this principle than the senate in this system; for the house of lords possess judicial powers, not only that of trying impeachments, but that of trying their own members, and civil causes when brought before them, from the courts of chancery, and the other courts in England.

If we therefore consider this constitution, with regard to this special object, though it is not so perfect as I would wish, yet it is more perfect than any other government that I know.

I proceed to another property which I think will recommend it to those who consider the effects of beneficence and wisdom. I mean the *division of this legislative authority* into two branches. I had an opportunity of dilating somewhat on this subject before. And as it is not likely to afford a subject of debate, I shall take no further notice of it, than barely to mention it. The next good quality, that I remark, is, that the *executive authority is one*; by this means we obtain very important advantages. We may discover from history, from reasoning and from experience, the security which this furnishes. The executive power is better to be trusted when it has no *screen*. Sir, we have a responsibility in the person of our president; he cannot act improperly, and hide either his negligence, or inattention; he cannot roll upon any other person the weight of his criminality: No appointment can take place without his nomination; and he is responsible for every nomination he makes. We secure *vigour*; we well know what numerous executives are.—We know there is neither vigour, decision nor responsibility in them. Add to all this—That officer is placed high, and is possessed of power, far from being contemptible, yet not a *single privilege* is annexed to his character; far from being *above the laws*, he is *amenable* to them in his *private character* as a *citizen*, and in his public character by impeachment.

Sir, it has often been a matter of surprise, and frequently complained of even in Pennsylvania, that the independence of the judges is not properly secured. The servile dependence of the judges, in some of the states, that have neglected to make proper provision on this subject, endangers the liberty and property of the citizen; and I apprehend that whenever it has happened, that the appointment has been for a less period than during good behaviour, this object has not been sufficiently secured—for if every five or seven years, the judges are obliged to make court for a re-appointment to office, they cannot be stiled independent. This is not the case with regard to those appointed under the general government. For the judges here shall hold their offices during good behaviour—I hope no further objections will be taken, against this part of the constitution, the consequence of which will be, that private property (so far as it comes before their courts)—and personal liberty, so far as it is not forfeited by crimes, will be guarded with firmness and watchfulness.

It may appear too professional to descend into observations of this kind, but I believe, that public happiness, personal liberty and private property, depend essentially upon the able and upright determinations of independent judges.

Permit me to make one more remark on the subject of the judicial department.—Its objects are extended *beyond* the bounds or power of every particular state, and therefore must be proper objects of the general government. I do not recollect any instance where a case can come before the judiciary of the United States, that could possibly be determined by a particular state, except one, which is, where citizens of the same state claim lands under the grant of different states, and in that instance, the power of the two states necessarily comes in competition; wherefore there would be great impropriety in having it determined by either.

Sir, I think there is another subject with regard to which this constitution deserves approbation.—I mean the *accuracy* with which the *line is drawn* between the powers of the *general government*, and that of the *particular state governments*. We have heard some general observations on this subject, from the gentlemen who conduct the opposition. They have asserted that these powers are unlimited and undefined. These words are as easily pronounced as limited and defined. They have already been answered by my honorable colleague (Mr. M'Kean) therefore, I shall not enter into an explanation; but it is not pretended, that the line is drawn with mathematical precision; the inaccuracy of language must, to a certain degree, prevent the accomplishment of such a desire. Whoever views the matter in a true light, will see that the powers are as minutely enumerated and defined as was possible, and will also discover, that the general clause, against which so much exception is taken, is nothing more, than what was necessary to render effectual the particular powers that are granted.

But let us suppose (and the supposition is very easy in the minds of the gentlemen on the other side) that there is some difficulty in ascertaining where the true line lies. Are we therefore thrown into despair? Are disputes between the general government, and the state governments, to be necessarily the consequence of inaccuracy? I hope, sir, they will not be the enemies of each other, or resemble comets in conflicting orbits mutually operating destruction. But that their motion will be better represented by that of the planetary system, where each part moves harmoniously within its proper sphere, and no injury arises by interference or opposition. Every part, I trust, will be considered as a part of the United States. Can any cause of distrust arise here? Is there any increase of risk? or rather are not the enumerated powers as well defined here, as in the present articles of confederation?

Permit me to proceed to what I deem another excellency of this system—all authority of every kind *is derived by*

REPRESENTATION *from the* PEOPLE, *and the* DEMOCRATIC *principle is carried into every part of the government*. I had an opportunity when I spoke first of going fully into an elucidation of this subject. I mean not now to repeat what I then said.

I proceed to another quality that I think estimable in this system---*it secures in the strongest manner the right of suffrage*. Montesquieu, book 2d, ch. 2d, speaking of laws relative to democracy, says, "when the body of the people is possessed of the SUPREME POWER, this is called a *democracy*. When the SUPREME POWER is lodged in the hands of a part of the people, it is then an *aristocracy*.

"In a democracy the people are in some respects the sovereign, and in others the subject.

"There can be no exercise of sovereignty but by their suffrages, which are their own will; now, the sovereign's will is the sovereign himself. The laws, therefore, which establish the right of suffrage, are fundamental to this government. And indeed it is as important to regulate, in a republic, in what manner, by whom, to whom, and concerning what, suffrages are to be given, as it is in a monarchy, to know who is the prince, and after what manner he ought to govern."

In this system it is declared, that the electors in each state shall have the qualification requisite for electors of the most numerous branch of the state legislature. This being made the criterion of the right of suffrage, it is consequently secured, because the same constitution *guarantees*, to every state in the union, a *republican* form of government. The right of suffrage is fundamental to republics.

Sir, there is another principle that I beg leave to mention---*Representation and direct taxation*, under this constitution, are to be according to numbers. As this is a subject which I believe has not been gone into in this house, it will be worth while to shew the sentiments of some respectable writers thereon. Montesquieu in considering the requisites in a confederate republic, book 9th, ch. 3d, speaking of Holland observes, "it is difficult for the United States to be all of equal power and extent. The Lycian[*] republic was an association of twenty-three towns; the large ones had three votes in the common council, the middling ones two, and the small towns one. The Dutch

[*] Strabo, lib. 14.

republic confists of seven provinces, of different extent of territory, which have each one voice.

The cities of Lycia ‡ contributed to the expences of the state, according to the proportion of suffrages. The provinces of the United Netherlands cannot follow this proportion; they must be directed by that of their power.

In Lycia § the judges and town magistrates were elected by the common council, *and according to the proportion already mentioned*. In the republic of Holland, they are not chosen by the common council, but each town names its magistrates. Were I to give a model of an excellent confederate republic, I should pitch upon that of Lycia.

I have endeavoured, in all the books that I could have access to, to acquire some information relative to the Lycian republic, but its history is not to be found; the few facts that relate to it are mentioned only by Strabo; and however excellent the model it might present, we were reduced to the necessity of working without it: give me leave to quote the sentiments of another author, whose peculiar situation and extensive worth, throws a lustre on all he says, I mean Mr. Neckar, whose ideas are very exalted both in theory and practical knowledge on this subject. He approaches the nearest to the truth in his calculations from experience, and it is very remarkable that he makes use of that expression; his words are,* " population can therefore be only looked on as an exact measure of comparison, when the provinces have resources nearly equal; but even this imperfect rule of proportion ought not to be neglected; and of all the objects which may be subjected to a determined and positive calculation, that of the taxes, to the population, approaches nearest to the truth."

Another good quality in this constitution is, that the members of the *legislature cannot hold offices under the authority of this government*. The operation of this I apprehend would be found to be very extensive, and very salutary in this country, to prevent those intrigues, those factions, that corruption, that would otherwise rise here, and have risen so plentiful in every other country. The reason why it is necessary in England to continue such influence, is that the crown, in order to secure its own influence against two other branches of the legislature, must continue to bestow places,

M

‡ Strabo. Lib. 14. § Ibid. * Neckar on Finance, Vol. 1. p. 308.

but those *places* produce the opposition which frequently runs so strong in the British parliament.

Members who do not enjoy offices, combine against those who do enjoy them. It is not from principle, that they thwart the ministry in all its operations. No; their language is, let us turn them out and succeed to their places.---The great source of corruption, in that country, is, that persons may hold offices under the crown, and seats in the legislature at the same time.

I shall conclude at present, and I have endeavoured to be as concise as possible, with mentioning, that in my humble opinion, the powers of the general government are necessary, and well defined---that the restraints imposed on it, and those imposed on the state governments, are rational and salutary, and that it is entitled to the approbation of those for whom it was intended.

I recollect, on a former day, the honorable gentleman from Westmoreland (Mr. Findley,) and the honorable gentleman from Cumberland (Mr. Whitehill) took exceptions against the first clause of the 9th sect. art. 1. arguing very unfairly, that because congress might impose a tax or duty of ten dollars on the importation of slaves, within any of the United States, congress might therefore permit slaves to be imported within this state, contrary to its laws.---I confess I little thought that this part of the system would be excepted to.

I am sorry that it could be extended no further; but so far as it operates, it presents us with the pleasing prospect, that the rights of mankind will be acknowledged and established throughout the union.

If there was no other lovely feature in the constitution, but this one, it would diffuse a beauty over its whole countenance. Yet the lapse of a few years ! and congress will have power to exterminate slavery from within our borders.

How would such a delightful prospect expand the breast of a benevolent and philanthropic European? Would he cavil at an expression? catch at a phrase? No, sir, that is only reserved for the gentleman on the other side of your chair to do. What would be the exultation of that great man, whose name I have just now mentioned, we may learn from the following sentiments on this subject: They cannot be expressed so well as in his own words. *

* Vol. 1. page 329.

"The colonies of France contain as we have seen, near five hundred thousand slaves, and it is from the number of these wretches, that the inhabitants set a value on their plantations. What a fatal prospect! and how profound a subject for reflection! Alas! how inconsequent we are, both in our morality, and our principles. We preach up humanity, and yet go every year to bind in chains twenty thousand natives of Africa! We call the Moors barbarians and ruffians, because they attack the liberty of Europeans, at the risque of their own; yet these Europeans go, without danger, and as mere speculators, to purchase slaves, by by gratifying the cupidity of their masters; and excite all those bloody scenes which are the usual preliminaries of this traffic! in short, we pride ourselves on the superiority of man, and it is with reason that we discover this superiority, in the wonderful and mysterious unfolding of the intellectual faculties; and yet a trifling difference in the hair of the head, or in the colour of the epidermis, is sufficient to change our respect into contempt, and to engage us to place beings like ourselves, in the rank of those animals devoid of reason, whom we subject to the yoke; that we may make use of their strength, and of their instinct, at command.

" I am sensible, and I grieve at it, that these reflections which others have made much better than me, are unfortunately of very little use! The necessity of supporting sovereign power has its peculiar laws, and the wealth of nations is one of the foundations of this power: thus the sovereign who should be the most thoroughly convinced of what is due to humanity, would not singly renounce the service of slaves in his colonies; time alone could furnish a population of free people to re-place them, and the great difference that would exist in the price of labour, would give so great an advantage to the nation that should adhere to the old custom, that the others would soon be discouraged in wishing to be more virtuous. And yet, would it be a chimerical project to propose a general compact, by which all the European nations should unanimously agree to abandon the traffic of African slaves! they would in that case, find themselves exactly in the same proportion relative to each other as at present; for it is only on comparative riches that the calculations of power are founded.

" We cannot as yet indulge such hopes; statesmen in

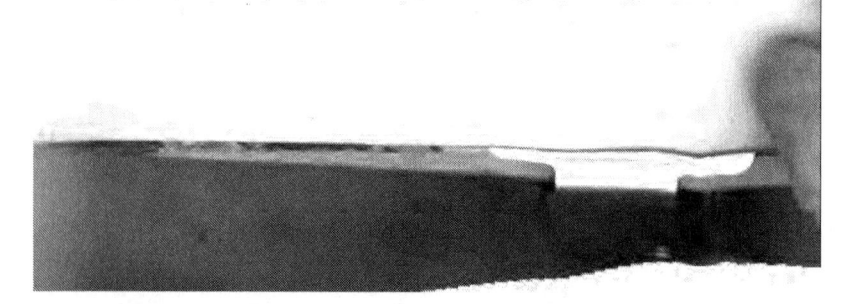

" general, think that every common idea muft be a low one;
" and fince the morals of private people ftand in need of
" being curbed, and maintained by the laws, we ought not
" to wonder, if thofe of fovereigns conform to their inde-
" pendence.

" The time may neverthelefs arrive, when, fatigued of
" that ambition which agitates them, and of the continual
" rotation of the fame anxieties, and the fame plans, they
" may turn their views to the great principles of humanity;
" and if the prefent generation is to be witnefs of this hap-
" py revolution, they may at leaft be allowed to be unani-
" mous in offering up their vows for the perfection of the
" focial virtues, and for the progrefs of public beneficial in-
" ftitutions," thefe are the enlarged fentiments of that
great man.

Permit me to make a fingle obfervation in this place on
the reftraints placed on the ftate governments; if only the
following lines were inferted in this conftitution, I think it
would be worth our adoption. "No ftate fhall hereafter
emit bills of credit;—make any thing, but gold and filver coin,
a *tender* in payment of debts; pafs any bills of attainder;
ex poft facto law; *or law impairing the obligation of contracts*.—
Fatal experience has taught us, dearly taught us! the value
of thefe reftraints.—What is the confequence even at this
moment? it is true we have no tender law in Pennfylvania;
but the moment you are conveyed acrofs the Delaware you
find it haunt your journey and follow clofe upon your heels.—
The paper paffes commonly at twenty five or thirty per cent.
difcount; how infecure is property!

Thefe are a few of thofe properties in this fyftem, that
I think recommend it to our ferious attention, and will
entitle it to receive the adoption of the United States.
Others might be enumerated, and others ftill will probably
be difclofed by experience.

FRIDAY, DECEMBER 7, 1787, A. M.

MR. WILSON.

This is the firft time that the article refpecting the judicial department, has come directly before us. I fhall therefore take the liberty of making fuch obfervations, as will
enable honorable gentlemen to fee the extent of the views

of the convention in forming this article, and the extent of its probable operation.

This will ennable gentlemen to bring before this houfe their objections more pointedly, than, without any explanation, could be done. Upon a diftinct examination of the different powers, I prefume it will be found, that not one of them is unneceffary. I will go further—there is not one of them but will be difcovered to be of fuch nature, as to be attended with very important advantages. I fhall beg leave to premife one remark, that the convention, when they formed this fyftem, did not expect they were to deliver themfelves, their relations and their pofterity, into the hands of fuch men, as are defcribed by the honorable gentlemen in oppofition. They did not fuppofe that the legiflature, under this conftitution, would be an *affociation of dæmons*: They thought that a proper attention would be given by the citizens of the United States, at the general election, for members to the houfe of reprefentatives; they alfo believed, that the particular ftates would nominate as good men as they have heretofore done, to reprefent them in the fenate. If they fhould now do otherwife, the fault will not be in congrefs, but in the people, or ftates themfelves. I have mentioned oftener than once, that for a people wanting to themfelves, there is no remedy.

The convention thought further (for on this very fubject, there will appear caution, inftead of imprudence in their tranfactions) they confidered, that if fufpicions are to be entertained, they are to be entertained with regard to the objects in which government have feparate interefts and feparate views, from the interefts and views of the people. To fay that officers of government will opprefs, when nothing can be got by oppreffion, is making an inferrence, bad as human nature is, that cannot be allowed. When perfons can derive no advantage from it, it can never be expected they will facrifice either their duty or their popularity.

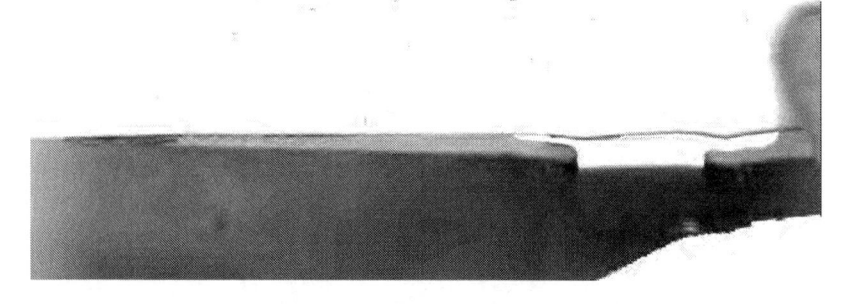

Whenever the general government can be a party againft a citizen, the trial is guarded and fecured in the conftitution itfelf, and therefore it is not in its power to opprefs the citizen. In the cafe of treafon, for example, though the profecution is on the part of the United States, yet the congrefs can neither define nor try the crime. If we have recourfe to the hiftory of the different governments that have hitherto fubfifted, we fhall find that a very great part of their tyranny over the people, has arisen from the extension of the definition of treason. Some very remarkable instances have occurred, even in so free a country as England. If I recollect right, there is one instance that puts this matter in a very strong point of view. A person possessed a favorite buck, and on finding it killed, wished the horns in the belly of the person who killed it; this happened to be the king; the injured complainant was tried and convicted of treason, for wishing the king's death.

I speak only of free governments, for in despotic ones, treason depends entirely upon the will of the prince. Let this subject be attended to, and it will be discovered where the dangerous power of the government operates to the oppression of the people. Sensible of this, the convention has guarded the people against it, by a particular and accurate definition of treason.

It is very true, that trial by jury is not mentioned in civil cases; but I take it, that it is very improper to infer from hence, that it was not meant to exist under this government. Where the people are represented—where the interest of government cannot be separate from that of the people, (and this is the case in trial between citizen and citizen) the power of making regulations with respect to the mode of trial, may certainly be placed in the legislature; for I apprehend that the legislature will not do wrong in an instance, from which they can derive no advantage. These were not all the reasons that influenced the convention to leave it to the future congress to make regulations on this head.

By the constitution of the different states, it will be found that no particular mode of trial by jury could be discovered that would suit them all. The manner of summoning jurors, their qualifications, of whom they should consist, and the course of their proceedings, are all different, in the different states; and I presume it will be allowed a good general principle, that in carrying into effect the laws of the general government by the judicial department, it will be proper to make the regulations as agreeable to the habits and wishes of the particular states as possible; and it is easily discovered that it would have been impracticable, by any general regulation, to have given satisfaction to all. We must have thwarted the custom of eleven or twelve, to have accommodated any one. Why do this, when there was no danger to be apprehended from the omission? We could not go into a particular detail of the manner that would have suited each state.

Time, reflection and experience, will be necessary to suggest and mature the proper regulations on this subject; time and experience were not possessed by the convention, they left it therefore to be particularly organized by the legislature—the representatives of the United States, from time to time, as should be most eligible and proper. Could they have done better?

I know in every part, where opposition has risen, what a handle has been made of this objection; but I trust upon examination it will be seen that more could not have been done with propriety. Gentlemen talk of bills of rights! What is the meaning of this continual clamour, after what has been urged, though it may be proper in a single state, whose legislature calls itself the sovereign and supreme power? yet it would be absurd in the body of the people, when they are delegating from among themselves persons to transact certain business, to add an enumeration of those things, which they are not to do. "But trial by jury is secured in the bill of rights of Pennsylvania; the parties have a right to trials by jury, which OUGHT to be held sacred," and what is the consequence? There has been more violations of this right in Pennsylvania, since the revolution, than are to be found in England, in the course of a century.

I hear no objection made to the tenure by which the judges hold their offices. It is declared that the judges shall hold them during good behaviour; nor to the security which they will have for their salaries. They shall at stated times receive for their services, a compensation which shall not be diminished during their continuance in office.

The article respecting the judicial department, is objected to as going too far, and is supposed to carry a very indefinite meaning. Let us examine this—the judicial power shall extend to all cases in law and equity, *arising under this constitution and the laws of the United States*. Controversies may certainly arise under this constitution and the laws of the United states, and is it not proper that there should be judges to decide them? The honorable gentleman from Cumberland (Mr. Whitehill) says, that laws may be made inconsistent with the constitution; and that therefore the powers given to the judges, are dangerous; for my part, Mr. President, I think the contrary inference true.

If a law should be made inconsistent with those powers vested by this instrument in congress, the judges, as a consequence of their independence, and the particular powers of government being defined, will declare such law to be null and void. For the power of the constitution predominates. Any thing therefore, that shall be enacted by congress contrary thereto, will not have the force of law.

The judicial power extends to all cases arising under treaties made, or which shall be made, by the United States. I shall not repeat, at this time, what has been said with regard to the power of the states to make treaties; it cannot be controverted, that when made, they ought to be observed. But it is highly proper that this regulation should be made; for the truth is, and I am sorry to say it, that in order to prevent the payment of British debts, and from other causes, our treaties have been violated, and violated too by the express laws of several states in the union. Pennsylvania, to her honor be it spoken, has hitherto done no act of this kind; but it is acknowledged, on all sides, that many states in the union have infringed the treaty; and it is well known, that when the minister of the United States made a demand of Lord Carmarthen, of a surrender of the western posts, he told the minister, with truth and justice, " The treaty, under " which you claim those possessions, has not been performed " on your part: Until that is done, those possessions will not " be delivered up." This clause, sir, will shew the world, that we make the faith of treaties a constitutional part of the character of the United States; that we secure its performance no longer nominally, for the judges of the United States will be enabled to carry them into effect, let the legislatures of the different states do what they may.

The power of the judges extends to all cases affecting ambassadors, other public ministers and consuls. I presume very little objection will be offered to this clause; on the contrary, it will be allowed proper and unexceptionable.

This will also be allowed with regard to the following clause, " all cases of admiralty and maritime jurisdiction."

The next is " to controversies to which the United States " shall be a party." Now I apprehend it is something very incongruous, that, because the United States are a party, it should be urged, as an objection, that their judges ought not to decide, when the universal practice of all nations have and unavoidably must admit of this power. But say the gentlemen, the sovereignty of the states is destroyed, if they should be engaged in a controversy with the United States, because a suitor in a court must acknowledge the jurisdiction of that court, and it is not the custom of sovereigns to suffer their names to be made use of in this manner. The answer is plain and easy: The government of each state ought to be subordinate to the government of the United States.

" To controversies between two or more states:" This power is vested in the present congress, but they are unable, as I have already shewn, to enforce their decisions. The additional power of carrying their decrees into execution, we find is therefore necessary, and I presume no exception will be taken to it.

" Between a state, and citizens of another state:" When this power is attended to, it will be found to be a necessary one. Impartiality is the leading feature in this constitution; it pervades the whole. When a citizen has a controversy with another state, there ought to be a tribunal, where both parties may stand on a just and equal footing.

" Between citizens of different states, and between a state, " or the citizens thereof, and foreign states, citizens or sub- " jects:" This part of the jurisdiction, I presume, will occasion more doubt than any other part, and at *first view* it may seem exposed to objections well-founded and of great weight; but I apprehend this can be the case only *at first view*. Permit me to observe here, with regard to this power, or any other of the foregoing powers given to the federal court, that they are not exclusively given. In all instances the parties may commence suits in the courts of the several states. Even the United States may submit to such decision if they think proper. Though the citizens of a state, and the citizens or subjects of foreign states, *may* sue in the fœderal court, it does not follow that they *must* sue. These are the instances in which the jurisdiction of the United States may be exercised; and we have all the reason in the world to believe, that it will be exercised impartially; for it would be improper to infer, that the judges would abandon their duty, the rather for being independent. Such a sentiment is contrary to experience, and ought not to be hazarded. If the people of the United States are fairly represented, and the president and senate are wise enough to choose men of abilities and integrity for judges, there can be no apprehension; because, as I mentioned before, the government can have no interest in injuring the citizens.

But when we consider the matter a little further, is it not necessary, if we mean to restore either public or private credit, that foreigners, as well as ourselves, have a just and impartial tribunal to which they may resort? I would ask, how a merchant must feel to have his property lay at the mercy of the laws of Rhode-Island? I ask further, how will a creditor feel, who has his debts at the mercy of tender laws in other states? It is true, that under this constitution, these particular iniquities may be restrained in future; but sir, there are other ways of avoiding payment of debts. There have been instalment acts, and other acts of a similar effect. Such things, sir, destroy the very sources of credit.

Is it not an important object to extend our manufactures and our commerce? This cannot be done, unless a proper security is provided for the regular discharge of contracts. This security cannot be obtained, unless we give the power of deciding upon those contracts to the general governments.

I will mention further, an object that I take to be of particular magnitude, and I conceive these regulations will produce its accomplishment. The object, Mr. President, that I allude to, is the improvement of our domestic navigation, the instrument of trade between the several states. That decay of private credit which arose from the destruction of public credit, by a too inefficient general government, will be restored, and this valuable intercourse among ourselves, must give an encrease to those useful improvements, that will astonish the world. At present, how are we circumstanced! Merchants of eminence will tell you, that they can trust their correspondents without law; but they cannot trust the laws of the state in which their correspondents live. Their friend may die, and may be succeeded by a representative of a very different character. If there is any particular objection that did not occur to me on this part of the constitution, gentlemen will mention it; and I hope when this article is examined, it will be found to contain nothing but what is proper to be annexed to the general government. The next clause, so far as it gives original jurisdiction in cases affecting ambassadors, I apprehend is perfectly unexceptionable.

It was thought proper to give the citizens of foreign states full opportunity of obtaining justice in the general courts, and this they have by its appellate jurisdiction; therefore, in order to restore credit with those foreign states, that part of the article is necessary. I believe the alteration that will take place in their minds, when they learn the operation of this clause, will be a great and important advantage to our country, nor is it any thing but justice; they ought to have the same security against the state laws that may be made, that the citizens have; because regulations ought to be equally just in the one case as in the other. Further, it is necessary, in order to preserve peace with foreign nations. Let us suppose the case, that a wicked law is made in some one of the states, enabling a debtor to pay his creditor with the fourth, fifth, or sixth part of the real value of the debt, and this creditor, a foreigner, complains to his prince or sovereign, of the injustice that has been done him: What can that prince or sovereign do? bound by inclination as well as duty to redress the wrong his subject sustains from the hand of perfidy, he cannot apply to the particular guilty state, because he knows that by the articles of confederation, it is declared that no state shall enter into treaties. He must therefore apply to the United States: The United States must be accountable: "My subject has received a flagrant injury; do me justice, or I will do myself justice." If the United States are answerable for the injury, ought they not to possess the means of compelling the faulty state to repair it? They ought, and this is what is done here. For now, if complaint is made in consequence of such injustice, congress can answer, "why did not your subject apply to the general court, where the unequal and partial laws of a particular state would have had no force?"

In two cases the supreme court has original jurisdiction; that affecting ambassadors, and when a state shall be a party. It is true, it has appellate jurisdiction in more, but it will have it under such restrictions as the congress shall ordain. I believe than any gentleman, possessed of experience or knowledge on this subject, will agree that it was impossible to go further with any safety or propriety, and that it was best left in the manner in which it now stands.

"In all the other cases before mentioned, the supreme court shall have appellate jurisdiction, both as to law and fact." The jurisdiction as to fact, may be thought improper, but those possessed of information on this head, see that it is necessary. We find it essentially necessary from the ample experience we have had in the courts of admiralty with regard to captures. Those gentlemen, who during the late war, had their vessels retaken, know well what a poor chance they would have had, when those vessels were taken into other states and tried by juries, and in what a situation they would have been, if the court of appeals had not been possessed of authority to reconsider and set aside the verdict of those juries. Attempts were made by some of the states to destroy this power, but it has been confirmed in every instance.

There are other cases in which it will be necessary; and will not congress better regulate them as they rise from time to time, than could have been done by the convention? Besides, if the regulations shall be attended with inconvenience, the congress can alter them as soon as discovered. But any thing done in convention, must remain unalterable, but by the power of the citizens of the United States at large.

I think these reasons will shew, that the powers given to the supreme court, are not only safe, but constitute a wise and valuable part of this system.

Tuesday, December 11, 1787, A. M.

Mr. Wilson.

Three weeks have now elapsed since this convention met: Some of the delegates attended on Tuesday the 20th November; a great majority within a day or two afterwards, and all but one on the 4th day. We have been since employed in discussing the business for which we are sent here. I think it will now become evident to every person who takes a candid view of our discussions, that it is high time our proceedings should draw towards a conclusion. Perhaps our debates have already continued as long, nay, longer than is sufficient for every good purpose. The business which we were intended to perform, is necessarily reduced to a very narrow compass. The single question to be determined is, shall we assent to and ratify the constitution proposed?

As this is the first state whose convention has met on the subject, and as the subject itself is of very great importance not only to Pennsylvania, but to the United States, it was thought proper, fairly, openly and candidly, to canvass it. This has been done. You have heard, Mr. President, from day to day, and from week to week, the objections that could be offered from any quarter. We have heard those objections once—we have heard a great number of them repeated much oftener than once. Will it answer any valuable end, sir, to protract these debates longer? I suppose it will not. I apprehend it may serve to promote very pernicious and destructive purposes. It may perhaps be insinuated to other states, and even to distant parts of this state, by people in opposition to this system, that the expediency of adopting, is at most very doubtful, and that the business labours among the members of the convention.

This would not be a true representation of the fact; for there is the greatest reason to believe, that there is a very considerable majority, who do not hesitate to ratify the constitution. We were sent here to express the voice of our constituents on the subject, and I believe that many of them expected to hear the echo of that voice before this time.

When I consider the attempts that have been made on this floor, and the many misrepresentations of what has been said among us that have appeared in the public papers, printed in this city, I confess that I am induced to suspect that opportunity may be taken to pervert and abuse the principles on which the friends of this constitution act. If attempts are made here, will they not be repeated when the distance is greater, and the means of information fewer? Will they not at length produce an uneasiness, for which there is, in fact, no cause? Ought we not to prohibit any such uses being made of the continuance of our deliberations? We do not wish to preclude debate—of this our conduct has furnished the most ample testimony. The members in opposition have not been prevented a repetition of all their objections, that they could urge against this plan.

The honorable gentleman from Fayette (Mr. Smilie) the other evening claimed for the minority, the merit of contending for the rights of mankind; and he told us, that it has been the practice of all ages, to treat such minorities with contempt: he further took the liberty of observing, that if the majority had the power, they do not want the inclination to consign the minority to punishment. I know that claims, self-made, form no small part of the merit, to which we have heard undisguised pretences; but it is one thing to claim, and it is another thing, very different indeed, to support that claim. The minority, sir, are contending for the rights of mankind; what then are the majority contending for? If the minority are contending for the rights of mankind, the majority must be contending for the doctrines of tyranny and slavery. Is it probable that that is the cafe? Who are the majority in this assembly? Are they not the people? are they not the representatives of the people, as well as the minority? Were they not elected by the people as well as by the minority? Were they not elected by the greater part of the people? Have we a single right separate from the rights of the people? Can we forge fetters for others, that will not be clasped round our own limbs? Can we make heavy chains, that shall not cramp the growth of our own posterity? On what fancied distinction shall the minority assume to themselves the merit of contending for the rights of mankind?

Sir, if the system proposed by the late convention, and the conduct of its advocates, who have appeared in this house, deserve the declarations and insinuations that have been made concerning them—well may we exclaim—Ill fated America! thy crisis was approaching! perhaps it was come! Thy various interests were neglected—thy most sacred rights were insecure. Without a government! without energy! without confidence internally! without respect externally! the advantages of society were lost to thee! In such a situation, distressed but not despairing, thou desiredst to re-assume thy native vigour, and to lay the foundation of future empire! Thou selectedst a number of thy sons, to meet together for the purpose. The selected and honored characters met; but horrid to tell! they not only consented, but they combined in an aristocratic system, calculated and intended to enslave their country! Unhappy Pennsylvania! thou, as a part of the union, must share in its unfortunate fate! for when this system, after being laid before thy citizens, comes before the delegates selected by you for its consideration, there are found but three of the numerous members that have virtue enough to raise their voices in support of the rights of mankind! America, particularly Pennsylvania, must be ill starred indeed, if this is a true state of the case! I trust we may address our country in far other language.

Happy America! thy crisis was indeed alarming, but thy situation was not desperate. We had confidence in our country; though on which ever side we turned, we were presented with scenes of distress. Though the jarring interests of the various states, and the different habits and inclinations of their inhabitants, all lay in the way, and rendered our prospect gloomy, and discouraging indeed, yet such were the generous and mutual sacrifices offered up, that amidst forty two members, who represented twelve of the United States, there were only three who did not attest the instrument as a confirmation of its goodness—happy Pennsylvania! this plan has been laid before thy citizens for consideration, they have sent delegates to express their voice; and listen, with rapture listen! from only three opposition has been heard against it.

The singular unanimity that has attended the whole progress of their business, will in the minds of those considerate men, who have not had opportunity to examine the general and particular interest of their country, prove to their satisfaction, that it is an excellent constitution, and worthy to be adopted, ordained and established by the people of the United States.

After having viewed the arguments drawn from *probability*, whether this is a good or a bad system, whether those who contend for it, or those who contend against it, contend for the rights of mankind, let us step forward and examine the *fact*.

We were told some days ago, by the honorable gentleman from Westmoreland (Mr. Findley) when speaking of this system and its objects, that the convention, no doubt, thought they were forming a compact or contract of the greatest importance. Sir, I confess I was much surprised at so late a stage of the debate, to hear such principles maintained. It was matter of surprise to see the great leading principle of this system, still so very much misunderstood. " The convention, no doubt, thought they were forming " a contract!" I cannot answer for what every member thought; but I believe it cannot be said, that they thought they were making a contract, because I cannot discover the least trace of a compact in that system. There can be no compact unless there are more parties than one. It is a new doctrine, that one can make a compact with himself. " The convention were forming compacts!" With whom? I know no bargains that were made there. I am unable to conceive who the parties could be. The state governments make a bargain with one another; that is the doctrine that is endeavoured to be established, by gentlemen in opposition; their state sovereignties wish to be represented! But far other were the ideas of the convention, and far other are those conveyed in the fyftem itfelf.

As this fubject has been often mentioned and as often mifunderftood, it may not be improper to take fome further notice of it. This, Mr. Prefident, is not a government founded upon compact; it is founded upon the power of the people. They exprefs in their name and their authority, "*We the People do ordain and eftablifh,*" &c. from their ratification, and their ratification alone; it is to take its conftitutional authenticity; without that, it is no more than *tabula rafa*.

I know very well all the common-place rant of ftate fovereignties, and that government is founded in original compact. If that pofition was examined, it will be found not to acceed very well with the true principle of free government. It does not fuit the language or genius of the fyftem before us. I think it does not accord with experience, fo far as I have been able to obtain information from hiftory.

The greateft part of government have been founded on conqueft; perhaps a few early ones may have had their origin in paternal authority. Sometimes a family united, and that family afterwards extended itfelf into a community. But the greateft governments which have appeared on the face of the globe, have been founded in conqueft. The great empires of Affyria, Perfia, Macedonia and Rome, were all of this kind. I know well that in Great-Britain, fince the revolution, it has become a principle, that the conftitution is founded in contract; but the form and time of that contract, no writer has yet attempted to difcover. It was however recognifed at the time of the revolution, therefore is politically true. But we fhould act very imprudently to confider our liberties as placed on fuch foundation.

If we go a little further on this fubject, I think we fee that the doctrine of original compact, cannot be fupported confiftently with the beft principles of government. If we admit it, we exclude the idea of amendment; becaufe a contract once entered into between the governor and governed, becomes obligatory, and cannot be altered but by the mutual confent of both parties. The citizens of United America, I prefume do not wifh to ftand on that footing, with thofe to whom, from convenience, they pleafe to delegate the exercife of the general powers neceffary for fuftaining and preserving the union. They wish a principle established, by the operation of which the legislatures may feel the direct authority of the people. The people possessing that authority, will continue to exercise it by amending and improving their own work. This constitution may be found to have defects in it; amendments hence may become necessary; but the idea of a government founded on contract, destroys the means of improvement. We hear it every time the gentlemen are up, " shall we violate the confederation, which directs every alteration that is thought necessary to be established by the state legislatures only." Sir, those gentlemen must ascend to a higher source; the people fetter themselves by no contract. If your state legislatures have cramped themselves by compact, it was done without the authority of the people, who alone possess the supreme power.

I have already shewn, that this system is not a compact or contract; the system itself tells you what it is; it is an ordinance and establishment of the people. I think that the force of the introduction to the work, must by this time have been felt. It is not an unmeaning flourish. The expressions declare, in a practical manner, the principle of this constitution. It is ordained and established by the people themselves; and we, who give our votes for it, are merely the proxies of our constituents. We sign it as their attornies, and as to ourselves, we agree to it as individuals.

We are told by honorable gentlemen in opposition, " that the present confederation should have been continued, but that additional powers should have been given to it: That such was the business of the late convention, and that they had assumed to themselves, the power of proposing another in its stead; and that which is proposed, is such an one as was not expected by the legislatures nor by the people. I apprehend this would have been a very insecure, very inadequate, and a very pernicious mode of proceeding. Under the present confederation, congress certainly do not possess sufficient power; but one body of men we know they are; and were they invested with additional powers, they must become dangerous. Did not the honorable gentleman himself tell us, that the powers of government, vested either in one man, or one body of men, formed the very description of tyranny? To have placed in the present, the legislative,

O

the executive and judicial authority, all of which are essential to the general government, would indubitably have produced the severest despotism. From this short deduction, one of these two things must have appeared to the convention, and must appear to every man, who is at the pains of thinking on the subject. It was indispensably necessary, either to make a new distribution of the powers of government, or to give such powers to one body of men, as would constitute a tyranny. If it was proper to avoid tyranny, it becomes requisite to avoid placing additional powers in the hands of a congress, constituted like the present; hence the conclusion is warranted, that a different organization ought to take place.

Our next enquiry ought to be, whether this is the most proper disposition and organization of the necessary powers. But before I consider this subject, I think it proper to notice one sentiment, expressed by an honorable gentleman from the county of Cumberland (Mr. Whitehill;) he asserts the extent of the government is too great, and this system cannot be executed. What is the consequence, if this assertion is true? It strikes directly at the root of the union.

I admit, Mr. President, there are great difficulties in adopting a system of good and free governments to the extent of our country. But I am sure that our interests as citizens, as states and as a nation, depend essentially upon an union. This constitution is proposed to accomplish that great and desirable end. Let the experiment be made; let the system be fairly and candidly tried, before it is determined that it cannot be executed.

I proceed to another objection; for I mean to answer those that have been suggested, since I had the honor of addressing you last week. It has been alleged by honorable gentlemen, that this general government possesses powers, for *internal* purposes, and that the general government cannot exercise internal powers. The honorable member from Westmoreland (Mr. Findley) dilates on this subject, and instances the opposition that was made by the colonies against Great-Britain, to prevent her imposing internal taxes or excises. And before the foederal government will be able to impose the one, or obtain the other, he considers it necessary that it should possess power for every internal purpose.

Let us examine these objections; if this government does not possess internal as well as external power, and that power for internal as well as external purposes, I apprehend, that all that has hitherto been done, must go for nothing. I apprehend a government that cannot anfwer the pupofes for which it is intended, is not a government for this country. I know that congrefs, under the prefent articles of confederation, poffefs no internal power, and we fee the confequences; they can recommend; they can go further, they can make requifitions; but there they muft ftop. For as far as I recollect, after making a law, they cannot take a fingle ftep towards carrying it into execution. I believe it will be found in experience, that with regard to the exercife of internal powers, the general government will not be unneceffarily rigourous. The future collection of the duties and impofts, will, in the opinion of fome, fupercede the neceffity of having recourfe to internal taxation. The United States will not, perhaps, be often under the neceffity of ufing this power at all; but if they fhould, it will be exercifed only in a moderate degree. The good fenfe of the citizens of the United States, is not to be alarmed by the picture of taxes collected at the point of the bayonet. There is no more reafon to fuppofe, that the delegates and reprefentatives in congrefs, any more than the legiflature of Pennfylvania, or any other ftate, will act in this manner. Infinuations of this kind, made againft one body of men, and not againft another, though both the reprefentatives of the people, are not made with propriety, nor will they have the weight of argument. I apprehend the greateft part of the revenue will arife from external taxation. But certainly it would have been very unwife in the late convention to have omitted the addition of the other powers; and I think it would be very unwife in this convention, to refufe to adopt this conftitution, becaufe it grants congrefs power to lay and collect taxes, for the purpofe of providing for the common defence and general welfare of the United States.

What is to be done to effect thefe great purpofes, if an impoft fhould be found infufficient? Suppofe a war was fuddenly declared againft us by a foreign power, poffeffed of a formidable navy, our navigation would be laid proftrate, our impofts muft ceafe; and fhall our exiftence as a nation, depend upon the peaceful navigation of our feas? A ftrong exertion of maratime power, on the part of an enemy, might deprive us of thefe fources of revenue in a few months. It may fuit honorable gentlemen, who live at the weftern extremity of this state, that they should contribute nothing, by internal taxes, to the support of the general government. They care not what restraints are laid upon our commerce; for what is the commerce of Philadelphia to the inhabitants on the other side the Alleghany Mountain? But though it may suit them, it does not suit those in the lower part of the state, who are by far the most numerous. Nor can we agree that our safety should depend altogether upon a revenue arising from commerce.

Excise may be a necessary mode of taxation; it takes place in most states already.

The capitation tax is mentioned as one of those that are exceptionable. In some states, that mode of taxation is used; but I believe in many, it would be received with great reluctance; there are one or two states, where it is constantly in use, and without any difficulties and inconveniences arising from it. An excise, in its very principles, is an improper tax, if it could be avoided; but yet it has been a source of revenue in Pennsylvania, both before the revolution and since; during all which time, we have enjoyed the benefit of free government.

I presume, sir, that the executive powers of government ought to be commensurate with the government itself, and that a government which cannot act in every part, is so far defective. Consequently it is necessary, that congress possess powers to tax internally, as well as externally.

It is objected to this system, that under it there is no sovereignty left in the state governments. I have had occasion to reply to this already; but I should be very glad to know at what period the state governments became possessed of the supreme power. On the principle on which I found my arguments, and that is the principle of this constitution, the supreme power resides in the people. If they chuse to indulge a part of their sovereign power to be exercised by the state governments, they may. If they have done it, the states were right in exercising it; but if they think it no longer safe or convenient, they will resume it, or make a new distribution, more likely to be productive of that good, which ought to be our constant aim.

The power both of the general government, and the state governments, under this system, are acknowledged to be so many emanations of power from the people. The great object now to be attended to, instead of disagreeing about who shall possess the supreme power, is to consider whether the present arrangement is well calculated to promote and secure the tranquillity and happiness of our common country. These are the dictates of sound and unsophisticated sense, and what ought to employ the attention and judgment of this honorable body.

We are next told, by the honorable gentlemen in opposition (as indeed we have been from the beginning of the debates in this convention, to the conclusion of their speeches yesterday) that this is a consolidated government, and will abolish the state governments. Definitions of a consolidated government have been called for; the gentlemen gave us what they termed definition, but it does not seem, to me at least, that they have as yet expressed clear ideas upon that subject. I will endeavour to state their different ideas upon this point. The gentleman from Westmoreland (Mr. Findley) when speaking on this subject, says, that he means by a consolidation, that government which puts the thirteen states into one.

The honorable gentleman from Fayette (Mr. Smilie) gives you this definition: " What I mean by a consolidated government, is one that will transfer the sovereignty from the state governments, to the general government.

The honorable member from Cumberland (Mr. Whitehill) instead of giving you a definition, sir, tells you again, that " it is a consolidated government, and we have proved it so."

These, I think, sir, are the different descriptions given us of a consolidated government. As to the first, that it is a consolidated government, that puts the thirteen United States into one; if it is meant, that the general government will destroy the governments of the states, I will admit that such a government would not suit the people of America: It would be improper for *this* country, because it could not be proportioned to *its extent* on the principles of freedom. But that description does not apply to the system before you. This, instead of placing the state governments in jeopardy, is founded on their existence. On this principle, its organization depends; it must stand or fall, as the state governments are secured or ruined. Therefore, though this may be a very proper description of a consolidating government, yet it must be disregarded as inapplicable to the proposed constitution. It is not treated with decency, when such insinuations are offered against it.

The honorable gentleman (Mr. Smilie) tells you, that a consolidating government, "is one that will transfer the sovereignty from the state governments to the general government." Under this system, the sovereignty is not in the possession of the state governments, therefore it cannot be transferred from them to the general government. So that in no point of view of this definition, can we discover that it applies to the present system.

In the exercise of its powers will be insured the exercise of their powers to the state government; it will insure peace and stability to them; their strength will encrease with its strength, their growth will extend with its growth.

Indeed narrow minds, and some such there are in every government—narrow minds, and intriguing spirits, will be active in sowing dissentions and promoting discord between them. But those whose understandings, and whose hearts are good enough to pursue the general welfare, will find, that what is the interest of the whole, must, on the great scale, be the interest of every part. It will be the duty of a state, as of an individual, to sacrifice her own convenience to the general good of the union.

The next objection that I mean to take notice of is, that the powers of the several parts of this government are not kept as distinct and independent as they ought to be. I admit the truth of this general sentiment. I do not think, that in the powers of the senate, the distinction is marked with so much accuracy as I wished, and still wish; but yet I am of opinion, that real and effectual security is obtained, which is saying a great deal. I do not consider this part as *wholly* unexceptionable; but even where there are defects in this system, they are improvements upon the old. I will go a little further; though in this system, the distinction and independence of power is not adhered to with entire theoretical precision, yet it is more strictly adhered to than in any other system of government in the world. In the constitution of Pennsylvania, the executive department exercises judicial powers, in the trial of public officers; yet a similar power in this system is complained of; at the same time the constitution of Pennsylvania is referred to, as an example for the late convention, to have taken a lesson by.

In New-Jersey, in Georgia, in South-Carolina, and in North Carolina, the executive power is blended with the legislative. Turn to their constitutions, and see in how many instances.

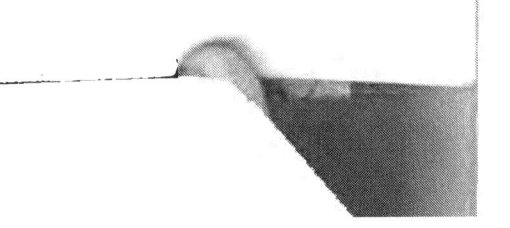

In North-Carolina, the senate and house of commons, elect the governor himself; they likewise elect seven persons, to be a council of state, to advise the governor in the execution of his office. Here we find the whole executive department, under the nomination of the legislature, at least the most important part of it.

In South-Carolina, the legislature appoint the governor and commander in chief, lieutenant governor and privy council. "Justices of the peace shall be nominated by the "legislature, and commissioned by the governor," and what is more, they are appointed during pleasure. All other judicial officers, are to be appointed by the senate and house of representatives. I might go further, and detail a great multitude of instances, in which the legislative, executive, and judicial powers are blended, but it is unnecessary; I only mention these to shew, that though this constitution does not arrive at what is called perfection, yet, it contains great improvements, and its powers are distributed with a degree of accuracy, superior to what is termed accuracy, in particular states.

There are four instances in which improper powers are said to be blended in the senate. We are told, that this government is imperfect, because the senate possess the power of trying impeachments. But here, sir, the senate are under a check, as no impeachment can be tried until it is made; and the house of representatives possess the sole power of making impeachments. We are told that the share which the senate have in making treaties, is exceptionable; but here they are also under a check, by a constituent part of the government, and nearly the immediate representative of the people, I mean the president of the United States. They can make no treaty without his concurrence. The same observation applies in the appointment of officers. Every officer must be nominated solely and exclusively, by the president.

Much has been said on the subject of treaties, and this power is denominated a blending of the legislative and executive powers in the senate. It is but justice to represent the favorable, as well as unfavorable side of a question, and from thence determine, whether the objectionable parts are of a sufficient weight to induce a rejection of this constitution.

There is no doubt, sir, but under this constitution, treaties will become the supreme law of the land; nor is there any doubt but the senate and president possess the power of making them. But though treaties are to have the force of laws, they are in some important respects very different from other acts of legislation. In making laws, our own consent alone is necessary. In forming treaties, the concurrence of another power becomes necessary; treaties, sir, are truly contracts, or compacts, between the different states, nations, or princes, who find it convenient or necessary to enter into them. Some gentlemen are of opinion, that the power of making treaties should have been placed in the legislature at large; there are, however, reasons that operate with a great force on the other side. Treaties are frequently, (especially in time of war,) of such a nature, that it would be extremely improper to publish them, or even commit the secret of their negociation to any great number of persons. For my part I am not an advocate for secrecy in transactions relating to the public; not generally even in forming treaties, because I think that the history of the diplomatique corps will evince, even in that great department of politics, the truth of an old adage, that "honesty is the best policy," and this is the conduct of the most able negociators; yet sometimes secrecy may be necessary, and therefore it becomes an argument against committing the knowledge of these transactions to too many persons. But in their nature treaties originate differently from laws. They are made by equal parties, and each side has half of the bargain to make; they will be made between us and the powers at the distance of three thousand miles. A long series of negociation will frequently precede them; and can it be the opinion of these gentlemen, that the legislature should be in session during this whole time? It well deserves to be remarked, that though the house of representatives possess no active part in making treaties, yet their legislative authority will be found to have strong restraining influence upon both president and senate. In England, if the king and his ministers find themselves, during their negociation, to be embarrassed, because an existing law is not repealed, or a new law is not enacted, they give notice to the legislature of their situation, and inform them that it will be necessary, before the treaty can operate, that some law be repealed, or some be made. And will not the same thing take place here? Shall less prudence, less caution, less moderation, take place among those who negotiate treaties for the United States, than among those who negotiate them for the other nations of the earth? And let it be attended to, that even in the making treaties the states are immediately represented, and the people mediately represented; two of the constituent parts of government must concur in making them. Neither the president nor the senate solely, can complete a treaty; they are checks upon each other, and are so balanced, as to produce security to the people.

I might suggest other reasons, to add weight to what has already been offered, but I believe it is not necessary; yet let me however add one thing, the senate is a favorite with many of the states, and it was with difficulty that these checks could be procured; it was one of the last exertions of conciliation, in the late convention, that obtained them.

It has been alleged, as a consequence of the small number of representatives, that they will not know as intimately as they ought, the interests, inclinations, or habits, of their constituents.

We find on an examination of all its parts, that the objects of this government are such, as extend beyond the bounds of the particular states. This is the line of distinction between this government, and the particular state governments.

This principle I had an opportunity of illustrating on a former occasion. Now when we come to consider the objects of this government, we shall find, that in making our choice of a proper character, to be a member of the house of representatives, we ought to fix on one, whose mind and heart are enlarged; who possesses a general knowledge of the interests of America, and a disposition to make use of that knowledge, for the advantage and welfare of his country. It belongs not to this government to make an act for a particular township, county, or state.

A defect in *minute* information, has not certainly been an objection in the management of the business of the United States; but the want of enlarged ideas, has hitherto been chargeable on our councils; yet even with regard to minute knowledge, I do not conceive it impossible to find eight characters, that may be very well informed as to the situation, interests and views, of every part of this state; and who may have a concomitant interest with their fellow citizens: they could not materially injure others, without affecting their own fortunes.

I did say, that in order to obtain that enlarged information in our representatives, a large district for election would be more proper than a small one. When I speak of large districts, it is not agreeable to the idea entertained by the honorable member from Fayette (Mr. Smilie) who tells you, that elections for large districts must be ill attended, because the people will not chuse to go very far on this business. It is not meant, sir, by me, that the votes should be taken at one place; no, sir, the elections may be held thro' this state, in the same manner as elections for members of the general assembly, and this may be done too without any additional inconvenience or expence.

If it could be effected, all the people of the same society ought to meet in one place, and communicate freely with each other on the great business of representation. Though this cannot be done in fact, yet we find that it is the most favorite and constitutional idea. It is supported by this principle too, that every member is the representative of the whole community, and not of a particular part. The larger therefore the district is, the greater is the probability of selecting wise and virtuous characters, and the more agreeable it is to the constitutional principle of representation.

As to the objection, that the house of representatives may be bribed by the senate, I confess I do not see that bribery is an objection against *this system*; it is rather an objection against human nature. I am afraid that bribes in every government may be offered and received; but let me ask of the gentlemen who urge this objection, to point out where any power is given to bribe *under this constitution?* Every species of influence is guarded against as much as possible. Can the senate procure money to effect such design? All public monies must be disposed of by law, and it is necessary that the house of representatives originate such law. Before the money can be got out of the treasury, it must be appropriated by law. If the legislature had the effrontery to set aside three or four hundred thousand pounds for this purpose, and the people would tamely suffer it, I grant it might be done; and in Pennsylvania the legislature might do the same; for by a law, and that conformably to the constitution, they might divide among themselves what portion of the public money they pleased. I shall just remark, sir, that the objections, which have repeatedly been made, with regard to " the number of reprefentatives being too fmall, and that they may poffibly be made fmaller; that the diftricts are too large, and not within the reach of the people; and that the houfe of reprefentatives may be bribed by the fenate." Thefe objections come with an uncommon degree of impropriety, from thofe who would refer us back to the articles of confederation. For under thofe, the reprefentation of this ftate cannot exceed feven members, and may confift of only two; and thefe are wholly without the reach or control of the people. Is there not alfo greater danger that the majority of fuch a body might be more eafily bribed, than the majority of one, not only more numerous, but checked by a divifion of two or three diftinct and independent parts? The danger is certainly better guarded againft in the propofed fyftem, than in any other yet devifed.

The next objections which I fhall notice, are, " that the powers of the fenate are too great, that the reprefentation therein is unequal, and that the fenate, from the fmallnefs of its number, may be bribed." Is there any propriety in referring us to the confederation on this fubject? Becaufe, in one or two inftances, the fenate poffefs more power than the houfe of reprefentatives, are thefe gentlemen fupported in their remarks, when they tell you they wifhed and expected more powers to be given to the prefent congrefs, a body certainly much more exceptionable than any inftituted under this fyftem?

" That the reprefentation in the fenate is unequal," I regret, becaufe I am of opinion, the ftates ought to be reprefented according to their importance; but in this fyftem there is confiderable improvement; for the true principle of reprefentation is carried into the houfe of reprefentatives, and into the choice of the prefident; and without the affiftance of one or the other of thefe, the fenate is inactive, and can do neither good or evil.

It is repeated again and again, by the honorable gentlemen, " that the power over elections, which is given to the general government in this fyftem, is a dangerous power." I muft own I feel myfelf furprized that an objection of this kind fhould be perfifted in, after what has been faid by my honorable colleague in reply. I think it has appeared by a minute inveftigation of the fubject, that it would have been not only unwife, but highly improper in the late convention, to have omitted this claufe, or given lefs power, than it does over elections. Such powers, fir, are enjoyed by every ftate government in the United States. In fome, they are of a much greater magnitude; and why fhould this be the only one deprived of them? Ought not thefe, as well as every other legiflative body, to have the power of judging of the qualifications of its own members? " The times, places and manner of holding elections for reprefentatives, may be altered by congrefs." This power, fir, has been fhewn to be neceffary, not only on fome particular occafions, but even to the very exiftence of the fœderal government. I have heard fome very improbable fufpicions indeed, fuggefted with regard to the manner in which it will be exercifed. Let us fuppofe it may be improperly exercifed; is it not more likely fo to be by the particular ftates, than by the government of the United States? becaufe the general government will be more ftudious of the good of the whole, than a particular ftate will be; and therefore, when the power of regulating the time, place or manner of holding elections, is exercifed by the congrefs, it will be to correct the improper regulations of a particular ftate.

I now proceed to the fecond article of this conftitution, which relates to the executive department.

I find, fir, from an attention to the arguments ufed by the gentlemen on the other fide of the houfe, that there are but few exceptions taken to this part of the fyftem. I fhall take notice of them, and afterwards point out fome valuable qualifications, which I think this part poffefs in an eminent degree.

The objection againft the powers of the prefident, is not that they are too many or too great, but to ftate it in the gentlemen's own language, they are fo trifling, that the prefident is no more than the *tool* of the fenate.

Now, fir, I do not apprehend this to be the cafe, becaufe I fee that he may do a great many things, independent of the fenate; and with refpect to the executive powers of government in which the fenate participate, they can do nothing without him. Now I would afk, which is moft likely to be the tool of the other? Clearly, fir, he holds the helm, and the veffel can proceed neither in one direction nor another, without his concurrence. It was expected by many, that the cry would have been againft the powers of the prefident as a monarchical power; indeed the echo of fuch found was heard, fome time before the rife of the late convention.

There were men at that time, determined to make an attack upon whatever syftem fhould be propofed, but they miftook the point of direction. Had the prefident phffeffed thofe powers, which the oppofition on this floor are willing to confign him, of making treaties, and appointing officers, with the advice of a council of ftate, the clamor would have been, that the houfe of reprefentatives, and the fenate, were the *tools* of the monarch. This, fir, is but conjecture, but I leave it to thofe who are acquainted with the current of the politics purfued by the enemies to this fyftem, to determine whether it is a reafonable conjecture or not.

The manner of appointing the prefident of the United States, I find is not objected to, therefore I fhall fay little on that point. But I think it well worth while, to ftate to this houfe, how little the difficulties, even in the moft difficult part of this fyftem, appear to have been noticed by the honorable gentlemen in oppofition. The convention, fir, were perplexed with no part of this plan, fo much as with the mode of choofing the prefident of the United States. For my own part, I think the moft unexceptionable mode, next after the one prefcribed in this conftitution, would be that practifed by the eaftern ftates, and the ftate of New-York; yet if gentlemen object, that an 8th part of our country forms a diftrict too large for elections, how much more would they object, if it was extended to the whole union? On this fubject, it was the opinion of a great majority in convention, that the thing was impracticable; other embarraffments prefented themfelves.

Was the prefident to be appointed by the legiflature? was he to continue a certain time in office, and afterward was he to become inelegible?

To have the executive officers dependent upon the legiflative, would certainly be a violation of that principle, fo neceffary to preferve the freedom of republics, that the legiflative and executive powers fhould be feparate and independent. Would it have been proper, that he fhould be apponted by the fenate? I apprehend, that ftill ftronger objections could be urged againft that—cabal—intrigue, corruption—every thing bad would have been the neceffary concomitant of every election.

To avoid the inconveniences already enumerated, and many others that might be fuggefted, the mode before us was adopted. By it we avoid corruption, and we are little exposed to the lesser evils of party and intrigue; and when the government shall be organized, proper care will undoubtedly be taken to counteract influence even of that nature—the constitution, with the same view has directed, that the day on which the electors shall give their votes, shall be the same throughout the United States. I flatter myself the experiment will be a happy one for our country.

The choice of this officer is brought as nearly home to the people as is practicable; with the approbation of the state legislatures, the people may elect with only one remove; for "each state shall appoint, in such manner as the legislature thereof may direct, a number of electors equal to the whole number of senators and representatives, to which the state may be entitled in congress." Under this regulation, it will not be easy to corrupt the electors, and there will be little time or opportunity for tumult or intrigue. This, sir, will not be like the elections of a Polish diet, begun in noise and ending in bloodshed.

If gentlemen will look into this article, and read for themselves, they will find, that there is no well-grounded reason to suspect the president will be the *tool* of the senate. "The president shall be commander in chief of the army and navy of the United States, and of the militia of the several states, when called into the actual service of the United States. He may require the opinion in writing of the principal officers in each of the executive departments, upon any subject relative to the duties of their respective offices; and he shall have power to grant reprieves and pardons, for offences against the United States." Must the president, after all, be called the *tool* of the senate? I do not mean to insinuate, that he has more powers than he ought to have, but merely to declare, that they are of such a nature, as to place him above expressions of contempt.

There is another power of no small magnitude, entrusted to this officer: "He shall take care, that the laws be faithfully executed."

I apprehend, that in the administration of this government, it will not be found necessary for the senate always to sit. I know some gentlemen have insinuated and conjectured, that this will be the case, but I am inclined to a contrary opinion. If they had employment every day, no doubt but it might be the wish of the senate, to continue their session; but from the nature of their business, I do not think it will be necessary for them to attend longer than the house of representatives. Besides their legislative powers, they possess three others, viz. trying impeachments—concurring in making treaties, and in appointing officers. With regard to their power in making treaties, it is of importance, that it, should be very seldom exercised—we are happily removed from the vortex of European politics, and the fewer, and the more simple our negotiations with European powers, the better they will be; if such be the case, it will be but once in a number of years, that a single treaty will come before the senate. I think, therefore, that on this account it will be unnecessary to sit constantly. With regard to the trial of impeachments, I hope it is what will seldom happen. In this observation, the experience of the ten last years support me. Now there is only left the power of concurring in the appointment of officers;—but care is taken, in this constitution, that this branch of business may be done without their presence—the president is authorised to fill up all vacancies, that may happen during the recess of the senate, by granting commissions, which shall expire at the end of their next session. So that on the whole the senate need not sit longer than the house of representatives, at the public expense; and no doubt if apprehensions are entertained of the senate, the house of representatives will not provide pay for them, one day longer than is necessary. But what (it will be asked) is this great power of the president? he can fill the offices only by temporary appointments. True; but every person knows the advantage of being once introduced into an office; it is often of more importance than the highest recommendation.

Having now done with the legislative and executive branches of this government, I shall just remark, that upon the whole of the executive, it appears that the gentlemen in opposition state nothing as exceptionable, but the deficiency of powers in the president; but rather seem to allow some degree of political merit in this department of government.

I now proceed to the judicial department; and here, Mr. President, I meet an objection, I confess I had not expected; and it seems it did not occur to the honorable gentleman (Mr. Findley) who made it, until a few days ago.

He alleges, that the judges, under this constitution, are not rendered sufficiently independent, because they may hold other offices; and though they may be independent as judges, yet their other office may depend upon the legiflature. I confefs, fir, this objection appears to me, to be a little wire-drawn in the firft place; the legiflature can appoint to no office, therefore the dependence could not be on them for the office, but rather on the prefident and fenate; but then thefe cannot add the falary, becaufe no money can be appropriated, but in confequence of a law of the United States. No finecure can be beftowed on any judge, but by the concurrence of the whole legiflature and of the prefident; and I do not think this an event that will probably happen.

It is true, that there is a provifion made in the conftitution of Pennfylvania, that the judges fhall not be allowed to hold any other office whatfoever; and I believe they are exprefsly forbidden to fet in congrefs; but this, fir, is not introduced as a principle into this conftitution. There are many ftates in the union, whofe conftitutions do not limit the ufefulnefs of their beft men, or exclude them from rendering fuch fervices to their country, for which they are found eminently qualified. New-York, far from reftricting their chancellor or judges of the fupreme court, from a feat in congrefs, exprefsly provide for fending them there on extraordinary occafions. In Connecticut, the judges are not precluded from enjoying other offices. Judges from many ftates have fat in congrefs. Now it is not to be expected, that eleven or twelve ftates are to change their fentiments and practice on this fubject, to accommodate themfelves to Pennfylvania.

It is again alleged againft this fyftem, that the powers of the judges are too extenfive; but I will not trouble you, fir, with a repetition of what I had the honor of delivering the other day; I hope the refult of thofe arguments gave fatisfaction, and proved that the judicial were commenfurate with the legiflative powers; that they went no further, and that they ought to go fo far.

The laws of congrefs being made for the union, no particular ftate can be alone affected, and as they are to provide for the general purpofes of the union, fo ought they to have the means of making the provifions effectual, over all that country included within the union.

Eodem Die, 1787. P. M.

Mr. Wilson.

I shall now proceed, Mr. President, to notice the remainder of the objections that have been suggested, by the honorable gentlemen who oppose the system now before you.

We have been told, sir, by the honorable member from Fayette (Mr. Smilie) "that the trial by jury was *intended* to be given up, and the civil law was *intended* to be introduced into its place, in civil cases."

Before a sentiment of this kind was hazarded, I think, sir, the gentleman ought to be prepared with better proof in its support, than any he has yet attempted to produce. It is a charge, sir, not only unwarrantable, but cruel; the idea of such a thing, I believe, never entered into the mind of a single member of that convention; and I believe further, that they never suspected there would be found within the United States, a single person that was capable of making such a charge. If it should be well founded, sir, they *must* abide by the consequences, but if (as I trust it will fully appear) it is ill founded, then he or they who make it, *ought* to abide by the consequences.

Trial by jury forms a large field for investigation, and numerous volumes are written on the subject; those who are well acquainted with it may employ much time in its discussion; but in a country where its excellence is so well understood, it may not be necessary to be very prolix, in pointing them out. For my part, I shall confine myself to a few observations in reply to the objections that have been suggested.

The member from Fayette (Mr. Smilie) has laboured to infer, that under the articles of confederation, the congress possessed no appellate jurisdiction; but this being decided against him, by the words of that instrument, by which is granted to congress the power of "establishing courts for receiving and determining, finally, appeals in all cases of capture;" he next attempts a distinction, and allows the power of appealing from the decisions of the judges, but not from the verdict of a jury; but this is determined against him also, by the practice of the states; for in every instance which has occurred, this power has been claimed by congress, and exercised by the court of appeals; but what would be the consequence of allowing the doctrine for which he contends? Would it not be in the power of a jury, by their verdict, to involve the whole union in a war? They may condemn the property of a natural, or otherwise infringe the law of nations; in this case ought their verdict to be without revisal? Nothing can be inferred from this, to prove that trials by jury were intended to be given up. In Massachusetts, and all the eastern states, their causes are tried by juries, though they acknowledge the appellate jurisdiction of congress.

I think I am not now to learn the advantages of a trial by jury; it has excellencies that entitle it to a superiority over any other mode, in cases to which it is applicable.

Where jurors can be acquainted with the characters of the parties, and the witnesses, where the whole cause can be brought within their knowledge and their view, I know no mode of investigation equal to that by a jury; they hear every thing that is alleged; they not only hear the words, but they see and mark the features of the countenance; they can judge of weight due to such testimony; and moreover, it is a cheap and expeditious manner of distributing justice. There is another advantage annexed to the trial by jury; the jurors may indeed return a mistaken, or ill founded verdict, but their errors cannot be systematical.

Let us apply these observations to the objects of the judicial department, under this constitution. I think it has been shewn already, that they all extend beyond the bounds of any particular state; but further, a great number of the civil causes there enumerated, depend either upon the law of nations, or the marine law, that is, the general law of mercantile countries. Now, sir, in such causes, I presume it will not be pretended that this mode of decision ought to be adopted; for the law with regard to them is the same here as in every other country, and ought to be administered in the same manner. There are instances, in which I think it highly probable, that the trial by jury will be found proper; and if it is highly probable that it will be found proper, is it not equally probable, that it will be adopted? There may be causes depending between citizens of different states, and as trial by jury is known and regarded in all the states, they will certainly prefer that mode of trial before any other. The congress will have the power of making proper regulations on is subject, but it was impossible for the convention to have gone minutely into it; but if they could, it muſt have been very improper, becauſe alterations, as I obſerved before, might have been neceſſary; and whatever the convention might have done would have continued unaltered, unleſs by an alteration of the conſtitution. Beſides; there was another difficulty with regard to this ſubject. In ſome of the ſtates they have courts of chancery, and other appellate juriſdictions, and thoſe ſtates are as attached to that mode of diſtributing juſtice, as thoſe that have none are to theirs.

I have deſired, repeatedly, that honorable gentlemen, who find fault, would be good enough to point out what they deem to be an improvement. The member from Weſtmoreland (Mr. Findley) tells us, that the trial between citizens of different ſtates, ought to be by a jury of that ſtate in which the cauſe of action aroſe. Now it is eaſy to ſee, that in many inſtances, this would be very improper and very partial; for beſide the different manner of collecting and forming juries in the ſeveral ſtates, the plaintiff comes from another ſtate; he comes a ſtranger, unknown as to his character or mode of life, while the other party is in the midſt of his friends, or perhaps his dependants. Would a trial by jury in ſuch a caſe enſure juſtice to the ſtranger? But again; I would aſk that gentleman, whether, if a great part of his fortune was in the hands of ſome perſon in Rhode-Iſland, he would wiſh, that his action to recover it, ſhould be determined by a jury of that country, under its preſent circumſtances?

The gentleman from Fayette (Mr. Smilie) ſays, that if the convention found themſelves embarraſſed, at leaſt they might have done thus much, they ſhould have declared, that the ſubſtance ſhould be ſecured by congreſs; this would be ſaying nothing unleſs the caſes were particularized.

Mr. Smilie.

I ſaid the convention ought to have declared, that the legiſlature ſhould eſtabliſh the trial by jury by proper regulations.

Mr. Wilson.

The legiſlature ſhall eſtabliſh it by proper regulations! So after all, the gentleman has landed us at the very point from which we ſet out. He wiſhes them to do the very thing they have done, to leave it to the diſcretion of congreſs. The fact, ſir, is, nothing more could be done.

It is well known, that there are some cases that should not come before juries; there are others, that in some of the states, never come before juries, and in these states where they do come before them, appeals are found necessary, the facts re-examined, and the verdict of the jury sometimes is set aside; but I think in all cases, where the cause has come originally before a jury, that the last examination ought to be before a jury likewise.

The power of having appellate jurisdiction, as to facts, has been insisted upon as a proof, " that the convention *intended* to give up the trial by jury in civil cases, and to introduce the civil law." I have already declared my own opinion on this point, and have shewn, nor merely, that it is founded on reason and authority. The express declaration of congress* is to the same purpose: They insist upon this power, as requisite to preserve the peace of the union; certainly, therefore, it ought always to be possessed by the head of the confederacy.

We are told, as an additional proof, that the trial by jury was intended to be given up, " that appeals are unknown to the common law; that the term is a civil law term, and with it the civil law is intended to be introduced." I confess I was a good deal surprized at this observation being made; for Blackstone, in the very volume which the honorable member (Mr. Smilie) had in his hand, and read us several extracts from, has a chapter entitled " of proceeding in the nature of appeals;" and in that chapter says, that the principal method of redress for erroneous judgments, in the king's courts of record, is by writ of error to some superior " *court of appeal*." § Now, it is well known, that his book is a commentary upon the common law. Here then is a strong refutation of the assertion, " that appeals are unknown to the common law."

I think these were all the circumstances adduced to shew the truth of the assertion, that in this constitution, the trial by jury was *intended* to be given up by the late convention in framing it. Has the assertion been proved? I say not, and the allegations offered, if they apply at all, apply in a contrary direction. I am glad that this objection has been stated, because it is a subject upon which the enemies of this constitution have much insisted. We have now had an opportunity of investigating it fully, and the result is, that there is no

* Journals of congress, March 6, 1779. § III. Blackstone, 406.

foundation for the charge, but it must proceed from ignorance, or something worfe.

I go on to another objection, which has been taken to this fyftem, "that the expence of the general government and of the ftate governments, will be too great, and that the citizens will not be able to fupport them." If the ftate governments are to continue as cumberfome and expenfive as they have hitherto been, I confefs it would be diftreffing to add to their expences, and yet it might be neceffary; but I think I can draw a different conclufion on this fubject, from more conjectures than one. The additional revenue to be raifed by a general government, will be more than fufficient for the additional expence; and a great part of that revenue may be fo contrived, as not to be taken from the citizens of this country; for I am not of opinion, that the confumer always pays the impoft that is laid on imported articles; it is paid fometimes by the importer, and fometimes by the foreign merchant who fends them to us. Had a duty of this nature been laid at the time of the peace, the greateft part of it would have been the contribution of foreigners. Befides, whatever is paid by the citizens, is a voluntary *payment*.

I think, fir, it would be very eafy and laudable, to leffen the expences of the ftate governments. I have been told, (and perhaps it is not very far from the truth) that there are *two thoufand* members of affembly in the feveral ftates; the bufinefs of revenue is done in confequence of requifitions from congrefs, and whether it is furnifhed or not, it commonly becomes a fubject of difcuffion. Now when this bufinefs is executed by the legiflature of the United States, I leave it to thofe who are acquainted with the expence of long and frequent feffions of affembly, to determine the great faving that will take place. Let me appeal to the citizens of Pennfylvania, how much time is taken up in this ftate every year, if not every feffion, in providing for the payment of an amazing intereft due on her funded debt. There will be many fources of revenue, and many opportunities for œconomy, when the bufinefs of finance fhall be adminiftered under one government; the funds will be more productive, and the taxes, in all probability, lefs burthenfome than they are now.

I proceed to another objection, that is taken againft the power given to congrefs, of raifing and keeping up ftanding armies. I confefs I have been furprized that this objection was ever made, but I am more fo that it is ftill repeated and infifted upon... I have taken fome pains to inform myfelf how the other governments of the world ftand with regard to this power; and the refult of my enquiry is, that there is not one which has not the power of raifing and keeping up ftanding armies. A government without the power of defence! it is a folecifm!

I well recollect the principle infifted upon by the patriotic body in Great-Britain; it is, that in time of peace, a ftanding army ought not to be kept up, without the confent of parliament. Their only apprehenfion appears to be, that it might be dangerous, was the army kept up without the concurrence of the reprefentatives of the people. Sir, we are not in the millenium. Wars may happen—and when they do happen, who is to have the power of collecting and appointing the force then become immediately and indifpenfably neceffary?

It is not declared in this conftitution, that the congrefs *fhall* raife and fupport armies. No, fir, if they are not driven to it by neceffity, why fhould we fuppofe they would do it by choice, any more than the reprefentatives of the fame citizens, in the ftate legiflatures? for we muft not lofe fight of the great principle upon which this work is founded. The authority here given to the general government, flows from the fame fource, as that placed in the legiflatures of the feveral ftates.

It may be frequently neceffary to keep up ftanding armies in time of peace. The prefent congrefs have experienced the neceffity; and feven hundred troops are juft as much a ftanding army as feventy thoufand. The principle which fuftains them is precifely the fame. They may go further, and raife an army, without communicating to the public the purpofe for which it is raifed. On a particular occafion, they did this: When the commotions exifted in Maffachufetts, they gave orders for enlifting an additional body of two thoufand men. I believe it is not generally known, on what a perilous tenure we held our freedom and independence at that period. The flames of internal infurrection were ready to burft out in every quarter; they were formed by the correfpondents of fome ftate officers (to whom an allufion was made on a former day) and from one end to the other of the continent, we walked on afhes, concealing fire beneath our feet; and ought congrefs to be deprived of power to prepare for the defence and fafety of our country? Ought they to be restrained from arming, until they divulge the motive which induced them to arm? I believe the *power* of raising and keeping up an army, in time of peace, is essential to every government. No government can secure its citizens against dangers, internal and external, without possessing it, and sometimes carrying it into execution. I confess it is a power, in the exercise of which all wise and moderate governments will be as prudent and forbearing as possible. When we consider the situation of the United States, we must be satisfied, that it will be necessary to keep up some troops for the protection of the western frontiers, and to secure our interest in the internal navigation of that country. It will be not only necessary, but it will be œconomical on the great scale. Our enemies finding us invulnerable, will not attack us, and we shall thus prevent the occasion for larger standing armies. I am now led to consider another charge that is brought against this system.

It is said, that congress should not possess the power of calling out the militia, to execute the laws of the union, suppress insurrections and repel invasions, nor the president have the command of them, when called out for such purposes.

I believe any gentleman who possesses military experience will inform you, that men without an uniformity of arms, accoutrements and discipline, are no more than a mob in a camp; that in the field, instead of assisting, they interfere with one another. If a soldier drops his musquet, and his companion, unfurnished with one, takes it up, it is of no service, because his cartridges do not fit it. By means of this system, a uniformity of arms and discipline will prevail throughout the United States.

I really expected that for this part of the system at least, the framers of it would have received plaudits, instead of censures, as they here discover a strong anxiety to have this body put upon an effective footing, and thereby, in a great measure, to supercede the necessity of raising, or keeping up, standing armies.

The militia formed, under this system, and trained by the several states, will be such a bulwark of internal strength, as to prevent the attacks of foreign enemies. I have been told, that about the year 1744, an attack was intended by France upon Massachusetts Bay, but was given up on reading the militia law of that province.

If a single state could deter an enemy from such attempts, what influence will the proposed arrangement have upon the different powers of Europe?

In every point of view, this regulation is calculated to produce the best effects. How powerful and respectable must the body of militia appear, under general and uniform regulations! how disjointed, weak and inefficient are they at present! I appeal to military experience for the truth of my observations.

The next objection, sir, is a serious one indeed; it was made by the honorable gentleman from Fayette (Mr Smilie) "The convention knew this was not a free government, otherwise they would not have asked the powers of the purse and sword." I would beg to ask the gentleman, what free government he knows that has not the powers of both? there was indeed a government under which we unfortunately were for a few years past, that had them not, but it does not now exist. A government without those powers, is one of the improvements with which opposition wish to astonish mankind.

Have not the freest government those powers? and are they not in the fullest exercise of them? this is a thing so clear, that really it is impossible to find facts or reason more clear, in order to illustrate it. Can we create a government without the power to act; how can it act without the assistance of men? and how are men to be procured without being paid for their services? is not the one power the consequence of the other?

We are told, and it is the last and heaviest charge, "that this government is an aristocracy, and was *intended* so to be by the late convention;" and we are told (the truth of which is not disputed) that an aristocratical government is incompatible with freedom. I hope, before this charge is believed, some stronger reasons will be given in support of it, than any that have yet been produced.

The late convention were assembled to devise some plan for the security, safety and happiness of the people of the United States; if they have devised a plan, that robs them of their power, and constitutes an aristocracy, they are the parricides of their country, and ought to be punished as such. What part of this system is it that warrants the charge?

What is an aristocratic government? I had the honor of giving a definition of it at the beginning of our debates; it is, fir, the government of a few over the many, elected by themfelves, or poffeffing a fhare in the government by inheritance, or in confequence of territorial rights, or fome quality independent of the choice of the people; this is an ariftocracy, and this conftitution is faid to be an ariftocratical form of government, and it is alfo faid that it was intended fo to be by the members of the late convention who framed it. What peculiar rights have been referved to any clafs of men, on any occafion? does even the firft magiftrate of the United States draw to himfelf a fingle privilege, or fecurity that does not extend to every perfon throughout the United States? Is there a fingle diftinction attached to him in this fyftem, more than there is to the loweft officer in the republic? Is there an office from which any one fet of men whatfoever are excluded? Is there one of any kind in this fyftem but is as open to the poor as to the rich? to the inhabitant of the country, as well as to the inhabitant of the city? and are the places of honor and emoluments confined to a few? and are thefe few the members of the late convention? Have they made any particular provifions in favor of themfelves, their relations, or their pofterity? If they have committed their country to the demon of ariftocracy, have they not committed themfelves alfo, with every thing they held near and dear to them?

Far, far other is the genius of this fyftem. I have had already the honor of mentioning its general nature; but I will repeat it, fir. In its principle, it is purely democratical; but its parts are calculated in fuch manner, as to obtain thofe advantages alfo, which are peculiar to the other forms of government in other countries. By appointing a fingle magiftrate, we fecure ftrength, vigour, energy and refponfibility in the executive department. By appointing a fenate, the members of which are elected for fix years, yet by a rotation already taken notice of, they are changing every fecond year, we fecure the benefit of experience, while, on the other hand, we avoid the inconveniences that arife from a long and detached eftablifhment. This body is periodically renovated from the people, like a tree, which, at the proper feafon, receives its nourifhment from its parent earth.

In the other branch of the legiflature, the houfe of reprefentatives, fhall we not have the advantages, of benevolence and attachment to the people, whofe immediate reprefentatives they are?

R

A free government has often been compared to a pyramid. This allusion is made with peculiar propriety in the system before you; it is laid on the broad basis of the people; its powers gradually rise, while they are confined, in proportion as they ascend, until they end in that most permanent of all forms. When you examine all its parts, they will invariably be found to preserve that essential mark of free governments—a chain of connection with the people.

Such, sir, is the nature of this system of government; and the important question at length presents itself to our view. Shall it be ratified, or shall it be rejected by this convention? In order to enable us still further to form a judgment on this truly momentous and interesting point, on which all we have or can have dear to us on earth, is materially depending, let us for a moment consider the consequences that will result from one or the other measure. Suppose we reject this system of government, what will be the consequence? Let the farmer say, he whose produce remains unasked for; nor can he find a single market for its consumption, though his fields are blessed with luxuriant abundance. Let the manufacturer and let the mechanic say, they can feel and tell their feelings. Go along the wharves of Philadelphia, and observe the melancholy silence that reigns. I appeal not to those who enjoy places and abundance under the present government; they may well dilate upon the easy and happy situation of our country. Let the merchants tell you, what is our commerce; let them say, what has been their situation, since the return of peace: An æra which they might have expected would furnish additional sources to our trade, and a continuance, and even an encrease to their fortunes. Have these ideas been realized, or do they not lose some of their capital in every adventure, and continue the unprofitable trade from year to year, subsisting under the hopes of happier times under an efficient general government? The ungainful trade carried on by our merchants, has a baneful influence on the interests of the manufacturer, the mechanic, and the farmer, and these I believe are the chief interests of the people of the United States.

I will go further—is there now a government among us that can do a single act, that a national government ought to do? Is there any power of the United States that can *command* a single shilling? this is a plain and a home question.

Congress may recommend, they can do more, they may

require, but they muſt not proceed one ſtep further.—If things are bad now, and that they are not worſe, is only owing to hopes of improvement, or change in the ſyſtem, will they become better when thoſe hopes are diſappointed? We have been told, by honorable gentlemen on this floor (Mr. Smilie, Mr. Findley and Mr. Whitehill) that it is improper to urge this kind of argument in favor of a new ſyſtem of government, or againſt the old one: unfortunately, ſir, theſe things are too ſeverely felt to be omitted; the people feel them; they pervade all claſſes of citizens, and every ſituation from New-Hampſhire to Georgia; the argument of neceſſity is the patriots defence, as well as the tyrant's plea.

Is it likely, ſir, that, if this ſyſtem of government is rejected, a better will be framed and adopted? I will not expatiate on this ſubject, but I believe many reaſons will ſuggeſt themſelves, to prove that ſuch expectation would be illuſory. If a better could be obtained at a future time; is there any thing eſſentially wrong in this? I go further, is there any thing wrong that cannot be amended more eaſily by the mode pointed out in the ſyſtem itſelf, than could be done, by calling convention after convention, before the organization of the government. Let us now turn to the conſequences that will reſult if we aſſent to, and ratify the inſtrument before you; I ſhall trace them as conciſely as I can, becauſe, I have treſpaſſed already too long on the patience and indulgence of the houſe.

I ſtated on a former occaſion one important advantage; by adopting this ſyſtem, we become a NATION; at preſent we are not one. Can we perform a ſingle national act? Can we do any thing to procure us dignity, or to preſerve peace and tranquillity? can we relieve the diſtreſs of our citizens? can we provide for their welfare or happineſs? The powers of our government are mere ſound. If we offer to treat with a nation, we receive this humiliating anſwer. "You cannot "in propriety of language make a treaty—becauſe you have "no power to execute it." Can we borrow money? There are too many examples of unfortunate creditors exiſting, both on this and the other ſide of the Atlantic, to expect ſucceſs from this expedient.—But could we borrow money, we cannot command a fund, to enable us to pay either the principal or intereſt; for, in inſtances where our friends have advanced the principal, they have been obliged to advance the interest also, in order to prevent the principal from being annihilated in their hands by depreciation. Can we raise an army? The prospect of a war is highly probable. The accounts we receive by every vessel from Europe, mention, that the highest exertions are making in the ports and arsehals of the greatest maritime powers; but, whatever the consequence may be, are we to lay supine? we know we are unable under the articles of confederation to exert ourselves, and shall we continue so, until a stroke be made on our commerce, or we see the debarkation of an hostile army on our unprotected shores? Who will guarantee that our property will not be laid waste, that our towns will not be put under contribution, by a small naval force, and subjected to all the horror and devastation of war? May not this be done without opposition, at least effectual opposition, in the present situation of our country? There may be safety over the Appelachian mountains, but there can be none on our sea coast. With what propriety can we hope our flag will be respected, while we have not a single gun to fire in its defence?

Can we expect to make internal improvement, or accomplish any of those great national objects, which I formerly alluded to, when we cannot find money to remove a single rock out of a river?

This system, sir, will at least make us a nation, and put it in the power of the union to act as such. We will be considered as such by every nation in the world. We will regain the confidence of our own citizens and command the respect of others.

As we shall become a nation, I trust that we shall also form a national character; and that this character will be adapted to the principles and genius of our system of government, as yet we possess none—our language, manners, customs, habits, and dress, depend too much upon those of other countries. Every nation in these respects should possess originality, there are not on any part of the globe finer qualities, for forming a national character, than those possessed by the children of America. Activity, perseverance, industry, laudable emulation, docility in acquiring information, firmness in adversity, and patience and magnanimity under the greatest hardships; from these materials, what a respectable national character may be raised! In addition to this character, I think there is strong reason to believe, that America may take the lead in literary improvements and national importance. This is a subject, which I confess, I have spent much pleasing time in considering. That language, sir, which shall become most generally known in the civilized world, will impart great importance over the nation that shall use it. The language of the United States will, in future times, be diffused over a greater extent of country, than any other that we now know. The French, indeed, have made laudable attempts toward establishing an universal language, but, beyond the boundares of France, even the French language is not spoken by one in a thousand. Besides, the freedom of our country, the great improvements she has made and will make in the science of government, will induce the patriots and literati of every nation, to read and understand our writings on that subject, and hence it is not improbable that she will take the lead in political knowledge.

If we adopt this system of government, I think we may promise security, stability and tranquility to the governments of the different states. They will not be exposed to the danger of competition on questions of territory, or any other that have heretofore disturbed them. A tribunal is here founded to decide, justly and quietly, any interfering claim; and now is accomplished, what the great mind of Henry the IV. of France had in contemplation, a system of government, for large and respectable dominions, united and bound together in peace, under a superintending head, by which all their differences may be accommodated, without the distruction of the human race!! We are told by Sully, that this was the favorite pursuit of that good king during the last years of his life, and he would probably have carried it into execution, had not the dagger of an assassin deprived the world of his valuable life. I have, with pleasing emotion, seen the wisdom and beneficence of a less efficient power under the articles of confederation, in the determination of the controversy between the states of Pennsylvania and Connecticut; but, I have lamented, that the authority of congress did not extend to extinguish, entirely, the spark which has kindled a dangerous flame in the district of Wyoming.

Let gentlemen turn their attention to the amazing consequences which this principle will have in this extended country—the several states cannot war with each other; the general government is the great arbiter in contentions between them; the whole force of the union can be called forth to reduce an aggressor to reason. What an happy exchange for the disjointed contentious state sovereignties!

The adoption of this system will also secure us from danger, and procure us advantages from foreign nations. This in our situation, is of great consequence. We are still an inviting object to one European power at least, and, if we cannot defend ourselves, the temptation may become too alluring to be resisted.—I do not mean, that, with an efficient government, we should mix with the commotions of Europe. No, sir, we are happily removed from them, and are not obliged to throw ourselves into the scale with any. This system will not hurry us into war, it is calculated to guard against it. It will not be in the power of a single man, or a single body of men, to involve us in such distress, for the important power of declaring war, is vested in the legislature at large;—this declaration must be made with the concurrence of the house of representatives; from this circumstance we may draw a certain conclusion, that nothing but our national interest can draw us into a war. I cannot forbear, on this occasion, the pleasure of mentioning to you the sentiments of the great and benevolent man whose works I have already quoted on another subject; Mr. Neckar, has adressed this country, in language important and applicable in the strictest degree to its situation and to the present subject. Speaking of war, and the great caution that all nations ought to use in order to avoid its calamities.—" AND you, rising nation, says he, whom generous efforts have freed from the yoke of Europe! let the universe be struck with still greater reverence at the sight of the privileges you have acquired, by seeing you continually employed for the public felicity: do not offer it as a sacrifice at the unsettled shrine of political ideas, and of the deceitful combinations of warlike ambition; avoid, or at least delay participating in the passions of our hemisphere; make your own advantage of the knowledge which experience alone has given to our old age, and preserve for a long time, the simplicity of childhood: in short, honor human nature, by shewing that when left to its own feelings, it is still capable of those virtues that maintain public order, and of that prudence which insures public tranquillity."

Permit me to offer one consideration more that ought to induce our acceptance of this system. I feel myself lost in the contemplation of its magnitude. By adopting this system, we shall probably lay a foundation for erecting temples of liberty, in every part of the earth. It has been thoug[ht] by many, that on the succefs of the ftruggle America h[as] made for freedom, will depend the exertions of the bra[ve] and enlightened of other nations.—The advantages refu[l]ting from this fyftem, will not be confined to the United Stat[es;] it will draw from Europe, many worthy characters, who pa[nt] for the enjoyment of freedom. It will induce princes, in o[r]der to preferve their fubjects, to reftore to them a porti[on] of that liberty of which they have for many ages been d[e]prived. It will be fubfervient to the great defigns of prov[i]dence, with regard to this globe; the multiplication of ma[n]kind, their improvement in knowledge, and their adva[nce]cement in happinefs.

Mr. M'KEAN.

SIR,

YOU have under your confideration a matter of very gr[eat] weight and importance, not only to the prefent generati[on] but to pofterity; for where the rights and liberties of [a] people are concerned, there certainly it is fit to proce[ed] with the utmoft caution and regard. You have done fo [hi]therto. The power of this convention, being derived fr[om] the people of Pennfylvania, by a *pofitive* and *voluntary* gra[nt,] cannot be extended farther than what this *pofitive gr*[ant] hath conveyed. You have been chofen by the people, [for] the fole purpofe of " affenting to and ratifying the confti[tu]tion, propofed for the future government of the Uni[ted] States, with refpect to their general and common concern[s,] or of rejecting it. It is a facred truft; and, as on the [one] hand, you ought to weigh well the innovations it will cre[ate] in the governments of the individual ftates, and the dang[er] which may arife by its adoption; fo upon the other ha[nd] you ought fully to confider the benefits it may promife, [and] the confequences of a rejection of it. You have hithe[rto] acted ftrictly conformably to your delegated power; [you] have agreed, that a fingle queftion can come bef[ore] you; and it has been accordingly moved, that you refol[ve] " to affent to and ratify this conftitution." Three we[eks] have been fpent in hearing the objections that have b[een] made againft it, and it is now time to determine, whet[her] they are of fuch a nature as to overbalance any benefit[s or] advantages that may be derived to the ftate of Pennfylv[ania] by your accepting it.

Sir, I have as yet taken up but little of your time; notwithstanding this, I will endeavour to contract what occurs to me on the subject: And in what I have to offer, I shall observe this method; I will first consider the arguments that have been used against this constitution, and then give my reasons, why I am for the motion.

The arguments against the constitution are, I think, chiefly these.

First. That the elections of representatives and senators are not frequent enough to ensure responsibility to their constituents.

Second. That one representative for thirty thousand persons is too few.

Third. The senators have a share in the appointment of certain officers, and are to be the judges on the impeachment of such officers. This is blending the executive with the legislative and judicial department, and is likely to screen the offenders impeached, because of the concurrence of a majority of the senate in their appointment.

Fourth. That the congress may by law deprive the electors of a fair choice of their representatives, by fixing improper times, places and modes of election.

Fifth. That the powers of congress are too large, particularly in laying internal taxes and excises, because they may lay excessive taxes, and leave nothing for the support of the state governments.

In raising and supporting armies, and that the appropriation of money for that use, should not be for so long a term as two years.

In calling forth the militia on necessary occasions; because they may call them from one end of the continent to the other, and wantonly harrass them: besides they may coerce men to act in the militia, whose consciences are against bearing arms in any case.

In making all laws which shall be necessary and proper for carrying into execution the foregoing powers, and all other powers vested by this constitution in the government of the United States, or in any department or officer thereof.

And in declaring, that this constitution, and the laws of the United States which shall be made in pursuance thereof, and all treaties made, or which shall be made, under the authority of the United States, shall be the supreme law land.

That migration or, importation of such persons, as any of the states shall admit, shall not be prohibited prior to 1808, nor a tax or duty imposed on such importation exceding ten dollars for each person.

Sixth. That the whole of the executive power is not lodged in the president alone, so that there might be one responsible person.

That he has the sole power of pardoning offences against the United States, and may therefore pardon traitors, for treasons committed in consequence of his own ambitious and wicked projects, or those of the senate.

That the vice-president is a useless officer, and being an excutive officer, is to be president of the senate, and in case of a division is to have the casting voice.

Seventh. The judicial power shall be vested in one supreme court. An objection is made, that the *compensation* for the services of the judges shall not be *diminished* during their continuance in office, and this is contrasted with the compensation to the president, which is to be neither *increased* nor *diminished* during the period for which he shall have been elected: But that of the judges may be increased, and the judge may hold other offices of a lucrative nature, and his judgment be thereby warped.

That in all the cases enumerated, except where the supreme court has original jurisdiction, " they shall have *appellate* jurisdiction, both as to law and facts, with such exceptions, and under such regulations as the congress shall make." From hence is inferred that the trial by jury is not secured.

That they have jurisdiction between citizens of different states.

Eighth. That there is no bill or declaration of rights in this constitution.

Ninth. That this is a *consolidation* of the several states, and not a *confederation*.

Tenth. It is an *aristocracy*, and was intended to be so by the framers of it.

The first objection that I heard advanced agaist this constitution, I say, sir, was that the elections of representatives and senators are not frequent enough to ensure responsibility to their constituents.

This is a subject that most men differ about, but there are more considerations than that of mere responsibility.

By this fystem the houfe of reprefentatives is compofed of perfons, chofen every fecond year by the people of the feveral ftates; and the fenators every fix years by the legiflatures: whether the one or the other of thefe periods are of too long duration, is a queftion to which various anfwers will be given; fome perfons are of opinion that three years in the one cafe, and feven in the other, would be a more eligible term, than that adopted in this conftitution. In Great-Britain, we find the houfe of commons elected for feven years; the houfe of lords is perpetual, and the king never dies. The parliament of Ireland is octennial, in various other parts of the Britifh dominions, the houfe of reprefentatives are during the royal pleafure, and have been continued twenty years; this, fir, is a term undoubtly too long. In a fingle ftate, I think annual elections moft proper, but then there ought to be more branches in the legiflature than one. An annual legiflature poffeffed of fupreme power, may be properly termed an annual defpotifm—and, like an individual, they are fubject to caprice, and act as party fpirit or fpleen dictates; hence that inftability to our laws, which is the bane of republican governments. The framers of this conftitution wifely divided the legiflative department, between two houfes fubject to the qualified negative of the prefident of the United States, tho' this government embraces only enumerated powers. In a fingle ftate, annual elections may be proper, the more fo, when the legiflative powers extend to all cafes; but in fuch an extent of country as the United States, and when the powers are circumfcribed, there is not that neceffity, nor are the objects of the general government of that nature as to be accquired immediately, by every capacity. To combine the various intereft of thirteen different ftates, requires more extenfive knowledge than is neceffary for the legiflature of any one of them; two years are therefore little enough, for the members of the houfe of reprefentatives to make themfelves fully acquainted with the views, the habits and interefts of the United Stats. With refpect to the fenate, when we confider the truft repofed in them, we cannot hefitate to pronounce, the period affigned to them is fhort enough; they poffefs, in common with the houfe of reprefentatives, legiflative power, with its concurrence they alfo have power to declare war; they are joined with the prefident in concluding treaties; it therefore behooves them to be converfant with the politics of the nations of the world, and the difpofitions of the fovereigns, and their minifters;—this requires much reading and attention. And believe me, the longer a man bends his ftudy to any particular fubject, the more likely he is to be mafter of it. Experience and practice will affift genius and education. I therefore think the time allowed, under this fyftem, to both houfes, to be extremely proper. This objection has been made repeatedly, but it can only have weight with thofe who are not at the pains of thinking on the fubject. When any thing, fir, new or great, is done, it is very apt to create a ferment among thofe out of doors, who as they cannot always enter into the depth and wifdom of counfels, are too apt to cenfure what they do not underftand; upon a little reflection and experience, the people often find that to be a fingular *bleffing* which at firft they deemed a *curfe*.

Second. "That one reprefentative for thirty thoufand perfons is too few."

There will be, fir, fixty five in the houfe of reprefentatives and twenty fix in the fenate, in all ninety one, who, together with the prefident, are to make laws in the feveral particular matters intrufted to them, and which are all enumerated and expreffed. I think the number fufficient at the prefent, and in three years time, when a cenfus or actual enumeration muft take place, they will be increafed, and in lefs than twenty five years they will be more than double. With refpect to this, different gentlemen in the feveral ftates will differ, and at laft the opinion of the majority muft govern.

Third. "The fenators have a fhare in the appointment of certain officers, and are to be the judges on the impeachment of fuch officers. This is blending the executive with the legiflative and judical department, and is likely to fcreen the offenders impeached, becaufe of the concurrence of a majority of the fenate in their appointment."

The prefident is to nominate to office, and with the advice and confent of the fenate appoint officers, fo that he is the refponfible perfon, and when any fuch impeachment fhall be tried, it is more than probable, that not one of the fenate, who concurred in the appointment, will be a fenator, for the feats of a third part are to be vacated every two years, and of all in fix.

As to the fenators having a fhare in the executive power, fo far as to the appointment of certain officers, I do not know where this restraint on the president could be more safely lodged. Some may think a privy-counsellor might have been chosen by every state, but this could little mend the matter if any, and it would be a considerable additional expence to the people. Nor need the senate be under any necessity of sitting constantly, as has been alleged, for there is an express provision made to enable the president to fill up all vacancies that may happen during their recess; the commissions to expire at the end of the next sessions.

As to impeachments, the objection is much stronger against the supreme executive council of Pennsylvania.

The house of lords in Great Britain, are judges in the last resort in all civil causes, and besides have the power of trying impeachments.

On the trial of impeachments the senators are to be under the sanction of an oath or affirmation, besides the other ties upon them to do justice; and the bias is more likely to be against the officer accused, than in his favor, for there are always more persons disobliged than the contrary when an office is given away, and the expectants of office are more numerous than the possessors.

"Fourth. That the congress may by law deprive the electors of a fair choice of their representatives, by fixing improper times, places and modes of election."

Every house of representatives are of necessity to be the judges of the elections, returns and qualifications of its own members. It is therefore their province, as well as duty, to see that they are fairly chosen, and are the legal members; for this purpose, it is proper they should have it in their power to provide, that the times, places and manner of election, should be such as to ensure free and fair elections.

Annual *congresses* are expressly secured; they have only a power given to them, to take care, that the *elections* shall be at convenient and suitable times and places, and conducted in a proper manner; and I cannot discover why we may not entrust these particulars to the representatives of the United States, with as much safety as to those of the individual states.

In some states the electors vote *viva voce*, in others by ballot; they ought to be uniform, and the elections held on the same day throughout the United States, to prevent corruption or undue influence. Why are we to suppose, that congress will make a bad use of this power, more than the representatives in the several states?

It is said " that the powers of congress, under this constitution, are too large, particularly in laying internal taxes and excises, because they *may* lay excessive taxes, and leave nothing for the support of the state governments." Sir, no doubt but you will discover, on consideration, the necessity of extending these powers to the government of the union. If they have to borrow money, they are certainly bound in honor and conscience to pay the interest, until they pay the principal, as well to the foreign as to the domestic creditor; it therefore becomes our duty to put it in their power to be honest. At present, sir, this is not the case, as experience has fully shewn. Congress have solicited and required the several states to make provision for these purposes; has one state paid its quota? I believe not one of them; and what has been the result? Foreigners have been compelled to advance money, to enable us to pay the interest due them on what they furnished to congress during the late war. I trust, we have had experience enough to convince us, that congress ought no longer to depend upon the force of requisition. I heard it urged, that congress ought not to be authorized to collect taxes, until a state had refused to comply with this requisition. Let us examine this position. The engagements entered into by the general government, render it necessary that a certain sum shall be paid in one year; notwithstanding this, they must not have power to collect it until the year expires, and then it is too late. Or is it expected that congress would borrow the deficiency? those who lent us in our distress, have little encouragement to make advances again to our government; but give the power to congress to lay such taxes as may be just and necessary, and public credit will revive; yet, because they have the power to lay taxes and excise, does it follow that they *must?* For my part, I hope it may not be necessary; but if it is, it is much easier for the citizens of the United States to contribute their proportion, than for a few to bear the weight of the whole principal and interest of the domestic debt; and there is perfect security on this head, because the regulation must equally affect every state, and the law must originate with the immediate representatives of the people, subject to the investigation of the state representatives. But is the abuse an argument against the use of power? I think it is not; and, upon the whole, I think this power wisely and secu[re lodged] in the hands of the general government; though on the first view of this work, I was of opinion they might have done without it; but, sir, on reflection, I am satisfied that it is not only proper, but that our political salvation may depend upon the exercise of it.

The next objection is against "the power of raising and supporting armies, and the appropriation of money for that use, should not be for so long a term as two years." Is it not necessary that the authority superintending the general concerns of the United States, should have the power of raising and supporting armies? are we, sir, to stand defenceless amidst conflicting nations? Wars are inevitable, but war cannot be declared without the consent of the immediate representatives of the people; there must also *originate* the law which appropriates the money for the support of the army, yet they can make no appropriation for a longer term than two years; but does it follow that because they *may* make appropriations for that period, that they *must* or even *will* do it? The power of raising and supporting armies, is not only necessary, but is enjoyed by the present congress, who also judge of the expediency or necessity of keeping them up. In England there is a standing army, though in words it is engaged but for one year, yet is it not kept constantly up? is there a year that parliament refuses to grant them supplies? though this is done annually, it might be done for any longer term. Are not their officers commissioned for life? and when *they* exercise this power with so much prudence, shall the representatives of this country be suspected the more, because they are restricted to two years?

It is objected that the powers of congress are too large, because "they have the power of calling forth the militia on necessary occasions, and may call them from one end of the continent to the other, and wantonly harrass them; besides they may coerce men to act in the militia whose consciences are against bearing arms in any case." It is true, by this system, power is given to congress to organize, arm, and discipline the militia, but every thing else is left to the state governments; they are to officer and train them: congress have also the power of calling them forth, for the purpose of executing the laws of the union, suppressing insurrections and repelling invasions; but can it be supposed they would call them in such case from Georgia to New-Hampshire? Common sense must oppose the idea.

Another objection was taken from these words of the constitution: "to make all laws which shall be necessary and proper for carrying into execution the foregoing powers, and all other powers vested by this constitution in the government of the United States, or in any department, or officer thereof." And in declaring "that this constitution, and the laws of the United States which shall be made in pursuance thereof, and all treaties made, or which shall be made, under the authority of the United States, shall be the supreme law of the land;" this has at last been conceeded, that though it is explicit enough, yet it gives to congress no further powers than those already enumerated. Those that first said it gave to congress the power of superceeding the state governments, cannot persist in it; for no person can, with a tolerable face, read the clauses over, and infer that such may be the consequence.

Provision is made that congress shall have power to prohibit the importation of slaves after the year 1808, but the gentlemen in opposition, accuse this system of a crime, because it has not prohibited them at once. I suspect those gentlemen are not well acquainted with the business of the diplomatic body, or they would know that an agreement might be made, that did not perfectly accord with the will and pleasure of any one person. Instead of finding fault with what has been gained, I am happy to see a disposition in the United States to do so much.

The next objections have been against the executive power; it is complained of, "because the whole of the executive power is not lodged in the president *alone*, so that there might be one responsible person; he has the *sole* powers of pardoning offences against the United States, and may therefore pardon traitors, for treasons committed in consequence of his own ambitious or wicked prospects, or those of the senate."

Observe the contradiction, sir, in these two objections; one moment the system is blamed for not leaving all executive authority to the president *alone*, the next it is censured for giving him the *sole* power to pardon traitors. I am glad to hear these objections made, because it forebodes an amendment in that body in which amendment is necessary. The president of the United States must nominate to all offices, before the persons can be chosen; he here consents and becomes liable. The executive council of Pennsylvania, appoint officers by ballot, which effectually destroys responsibility. He may pardon offences, and hence it is inferred that he may pardon traitors, for treason committed in consequence of his own ambitious and wicked projects. The executive council of Pennsylvania can do the same. But the president of the United States may be impeached before the senate and punished for his crimes.

"The vice-president is an useless officer;" perhaps the government might be executed without him, but there is a necessity of having a person to preside in the senate, to continue a full representation of each state in that body. The chancellor of England is a judicial officer, yet he sits in the house of lords.

The next objection is against the judicial department. The judicial power shall be vested in one supreme court. An objection is made that the compensation for the services of the judges shall not be *diminished* during their continuance in office, and this is contrasted with the compensation of the president, which is to be neither *encreased* nor *diminished*, during the period for which he shall be elected. But that of the judges may be encreased, and the judges may hold other offices of a lucrative nature, and his judgment be thereby warped.

Do gentlemen not see the reason why this difference is made? do they not see that the president is appointed but for four years, whilst the judges may continue for life, if they shall so long behave themselves well? In the first case, little alteration can happen in the value of money, but in the course of a man's life, a very great one may take place from the discovery of silver and gold mines, and the great influx of those metals; in which case an encrease of salary may be requisite. A security that their compensation shall not be lessened, nor they have to look up to every session for salary, will certainly tend to make those officers more easy and independent.

"The judges may hold other offices of a lucrative nature:" this part of the objection reminds me of the scheme that was fallen upon in Pennsylvania, to prevent any person from taking up large tracts of land: a law was passed restricting the purchaser to a tract not exceeding three hundred acres; but all the difference it made, was, that the land was taken up by several patents, instead of one, and the wealthy could procure, if they chose it, three thousand acres. What though the judges could hold no other office, might they not have brothers, children and other relations, whom they might wish to see placed in the offices forbidden to themselves? I see no apprehensions that may be entertained on this account.

That in all cases enumerated, except where the supreme court has original jurisdiction, "they shall have appellate jurisdiction both as to law and fact, with such exceptions and under such regulations as the congress shall make." From this is inferred, that the trial by jury is not secured; and an objection is set up to the system, because they have jurisdiction between citizens of different states. Regulations, under this head, are necessary, but the convention would form no one that would have suited each. of the United States. It has been a subject of amazement to me, to hear gentlemen contend that the verdict of a jury shall be without revision in all cases. Juries are not infallible because they are twelve in number. When the law is so blended with the fact, as to be almost inseperable, may not the decision of a jury be erroneous? Yet notwithstanding this, trial by jury is the best mode that is known. Appellate jurisdiction, sir, is known in the common law, and causes are removed from inferior courts by writ of error into some court of appeal. It is said that the lord chancellor, in all cases, sends down to the lower courts when he wants to determine a fact, but that opinion is not well-founded, because he determines nineteen out of twenty, without the intervention of any jury. The power to try causes between citizens of different states, was thought by some gentlemen invidious; but I apprehend they must see the necessity of it, from what has been already said by my honorable colleague.

"That there is no bill or declaration of rights in this constitution."

To this I answer, such a thing has not been deemed essential to liberty, excepting in Great-Britain, where there is a king and an house of Lords, quite distinct with respect to power and interest from the rest of the people; or in Poland, the *pacta conventa*, which the king signs before he is crowned, and in six states of the American United States.

Again, because it is unnecessary; for the powers of congress, being derived from the people in the mode pointed out by this constitution, and being therein enumerated and

T

positively granted, can be no other than what this positive grant conveys [*].

With respect to executive officers, they have no manner of authority, any of them, beyond what is, by *positive* grant and commission, delegated to them.

"That this is a *consolidation* of the several states, and not a *confederation* :"

To this I answer, the name is immaterial—the thing unites the several states, and makes them like one in particular instances and for particular purposes, which is what is ardently desired by most of the sensible men in this country. I care not, whether it is called a consolidation, confederation, or national government, or by what other name, if it is a good government, and calculated to promote the blessings of liberty, tranquillity and happiness.

"It is an *aristocracy*, and was intended to be so by the framers of it :"

Here again, sir, the name is immaterial, if it is a good system of government for the general and common concerns of the United States. But after the definition which has already been given of an aristocratic government, it becomes unnecessary to repeat arguments to prove that this system does not establish an aristocracy.

There have been some other small objections to, or rather criticisms on this work, which I rest assured the gentlemen who made them, will, on reflection, excuse me in omitting to notice them.

Many parts of this constitution have been wrested and tortured, in order to make way for shadowy objections, which must have been observed by every auditor. Some other things were said with acrimony ; they seemed to be personal ; I heard the sound, but it was inarticulate. I can compare it to nothing better, than the feeble noise occasioned by the working of small beer.

It holds in argument as well as nature, that *destructio unius est generatio alterius*—the refutation of an argument begets a proof.

The objections to this constitution having been answered, and all done away, it remains pure and unhurt, and this alone is a forcible argument of its goodness.

Mr. President, I am sure nothing can prevail with me to give my vote for ratifying this constitution, but a conviction

[*] *Locke on civil government, vol. 2, b. 2, chap. ii. sect. 141, and in the xiiith chap. sect. 152.*

from comparing the arguments on both sides, that the not doing it, is liable to more inconvenience and danger, than the doing it.

I. If you do it, you strengthen the government and people of these United States, and will thereby have the wisdom and assistance of all the states.

II. You will settle, establish and firmly perpetuate our independence, by destroying the vain hopes of all its enemies, both at home and abroad.

III. You will encourage your allies to join with you; nay to depend, that what hath been stipulated or shall hereafter be stipulated and agreed upon, will be punctually performed, and other nations will be induced to enter into treaties with you.

IV. It will have a tendency to break our parties and divisions, and by that means, lay a firm and solid foundation for the future tranquillity and happiness of the United States in general, and of this state in particular.

V. It will invigorate your commerce, and encourage shipbuilding.

VI. It will have a tendency not only to prevent any other nation from making war upon you, but from offering you any wrong or even insult.

In short, the advantages that must result from it, are obviously so numerous and important, and have been so fully and ably pointed out by others, that it appears to be unnecessary to enlarge on this head.

Upon the whole, sir, the law has been my study from my infancy, and my only profession. I have gone through the circle of office, in the legislative, executive and judicial departments of government; and from all my study, observation and experience, I must declare, that from a full examination and due consideration of this system, it appears to me the *best the world has yet seen.*

I congratulate you on the fair prospect of its being adopted, and am happy in the expectation of seeing accomplished, what has been long my ardent wish—that you will hereafter have a SALUTARY PERMANENCY, in *magistracy* and STABILITY IN THE LAWS.

ERRATA.

Page 34 line 13 for *disadvantages* read advantages.
  39   19 after prevalence, insert of this principle.
  58   15 *dele* these were the very expressions used in 1783.
  64   12 read for it *cannot* be amended.
        29 *but* because.
  69   19 governments.
  103   32 *compact*.
        34 idem.
  122   4 neutral.
        20 judge of *the* weight.

CPSIA information can be obtained
at www.ICGtesting.com
Printed in the USA
BVHW040548181019
561272BV00009B/109/P